The Metaphoric Structure
of *Paradise Lost*

THE
METAPHORIC
STRUCTURE OF
PARADISE LOST

BY JACKSON I. COPE

THE JOHNS HOPKINS PRESS
BALTIMORE

© 1962 by *The Johns Hopkins Press, Baltimore 18, Maryland*
Distributed in Great Britain by Oxford University Press, London

Printed in the United States of America
by The Haddon Craftsmen, Inc., Scranton

Library of Congress Catalog Card Number: 62-11709

This book has been brought to publication with the assistance of a grant from The Ford Foundation.

FOR DON CAMERON ALLEN

. . . si mosse, ed io li tenni retro.

Acknowledgments

THIS BOOK GREW out of the pleasure of reading Milton with good students in seminars at Washington University and at Rice University; in particular, I thank Cooper Mackin, Roy Roussel and Ray Waddington, friends who encouraged with their rage for order . . . keener sounds.

A summer fellowship at the Folger Shakespeare Library provided me with the time to write it all down; funds from Rice University expedited the final preparation of the manuscript. By permission of the Odyssey Press, the text employed in citing *Paradise Lost* is that edited by Merritt Y. Hughes.

Fragments of what follows have appeared in *ELH, Modern Philology* (University of Chicago Press), and *PMLA*; I owe the editors of these journals a debt of gratitude both for their careful assistance and for their kind permission to reprint material.

Don Cameron Allen, Albert J. Kuhn, Arnold Stein, and Aubrey Williams have at various times read and left large marks upon the whole; there were many lapses of detail and of perspective which their patience has erased, while the others my obstinacy retained. Aubrey will know why I must single him out with special thanks for good comfort which extended far beyond the limits of these pages while they were being written.

Contents

I

POETS AND CRITICS: The Metaphoric School

NO OBSERVER OF the Renaissance need be told that literary criticism in recent years has removed its focal interest from John Donne and the Metaphysical poets to John Milton. The movement is discernible even amidst an increasing deluge of critical studies and reprints flooding into every channel of interest. As readings of the great Puritan proliferate, we have already received a history of the Metaphysical revival which, like all histories, is something of an epitaph.[1]

One observes further that this shift has been closely paralleled by another: I speak of the truism that almost without our noticing, the once flourishing *explication de textes* has become largely a classroom exercise, having resigned the public stage of print except for occasional dazzling performances in historical garb.[2]

[1] Joseph E. Duncan, *The Revival of Metaphysical Poetry: The History of a Style, 1800 to the Present* (Minneapolis, 1959). A considerably less ambitious precursor was Sona Raiziss, *The Metaphysical Passion* (Philadelphia, 1952). Most recently, Arnold Stein has acknowledged the passing of interest in Donne from its apogee in a public defense of another generation's taste. See "Donne and the 1920's: A Problem in Historical Consciousness," *ELH*, XXVII (1960), 16-29.

[2] This fact is mirrored in the gradual retirement from the critical scene of the "New Critics," those men whose names became most closely associated

Despite earlier hints, such as Eliot's tercentenary warning that Donne's poetry might be "a concern of the present and the recent past, rather than of the future,"[3] the effective end of the Metaphysicals' domination of taste can be demarcated, more sharply than is usual in such matters, at the publication of Louis L. Martz' *Poetry of Meditation* in 1954. Since then there has appeared no new book of criticism concerned exclusively either with Donne or with the Metaphysical group. Rather, effort has been directed toward making those critical distinctions which would separate such contemporaries as George Herbert or Henry

---

with the explicatory method in America. William Empson, the most talented and therefore most elusive of the pleiad of the thirties and forties, is an instructive exception. Primarily a textural rather than a contextual critic, he dealt extensively with Milton in *Some Versions of Pastoral* (New York, 1950; the original American edition [1938] bore the title *English Pastoral Poetry*), and briefly in *The Structure of Complex Words* (New York, 1951). As I write, there is announcement of his forthcoming book titled *Milton's God*. Not only is Empson still very active, but he is the only man associated with the rise of the New Criticism who has seriously and extensively attended to *Paradise Lost*. Cleanth Brooks followed Eliot in the post-1948 revaluation period with work chiefly on the early poems, but his point was not greatly instructive, i.e., that Milton used metaphor "organically" and, hence, shared common bearings with Donne. See his essays "Milton and the New Criticism," *SR*, LIX (1951), 1-22, and "Milton and Critical Re-estimates," *PMLA*, LXVI (1951), 1045-54. His major effort (in collaboration with John Hardy) was the series of explications in *Poems of Mr. John Milton: the 1645 Edition with Essays in Analysis* (New York, 1951). John Crowe Ransom treated *Paradise Lost* and *Paradise Regained* as parables of the effects of secularism and scientism, not at all as literary works, in his early *God Without Thunder: An Unorthodox Defense of Orthodoxy* (New York, 1930), pp. 127-38, 141-6. As critic he dealt with *Lycidas* in the best single Miltonic essay written by a member of this group: "A Poem Nearly Anonymous," *American Review*, I (1933), 179-203. M. K. Starkman, "The Militant Miltonist; or, The Retreat from Humanism," *ELH*, XXVI (1959), 209-28, examines the apologetic rather than aesthetic ends that underlie most of the abortive attempts to draw Milton into the New Critical fold; and Herbert Howarth, "Eliot and Milton: The American Aspect," *UTQ*, XXX (1961), 150-62, carefully analyzes Eliot's attitudes toward Milton as a mirror-image of his attitudes toward a Harvard-oriented "Puritan" tradition.

[3] "Donne in Our Time," in *A Garland for John Donne*, ed. Theodore Spencer (Cambridge, Mass., 1931), p. 5.

Vaughan from the master. On the other hand, until 1953 there had been no books on Milton employing the methods of detailed analysis which have become the hallmark of twentieth-century criticism, if we except the rather ephemeral series by E. M. W. Tillyard and that by B. Rajan.[4]

However, within a few months of Martz' study, Arnold Stein, Don Cameron Allen and W. B. C. Watkins each issued percep- tive book-length examinations of Milton as poet. They were quickly followed by the iconoclastic but often creative endeavor of Robert Martin Adams in 1955; by the handsomely docu- mented readings of Howard Schultz and Kester Svendsen in that and the following year; by Stein's elaborate analysis of the later poems in a 1957 volume which appeared almost simul- taneously with Rosemond Tuve's essay into the imagery of earlier pieces; and most recently by Isabel MacCaffrey's im- portant *Paradise Lost as "Myth,"* as well as by the thematically less coherent, more impressionistic readings of *Paradise Lost* by J. B. Broadbent and by John Peter.[5]

---

[4] Tillyard's studies made only occasional critical flourishes, and are best classified as extensions of Raleigh's *Milton* overlaid with unintentional parodies of Freudian biography: see *Milton* (London, 1930), *The Miltonic Setting* (London, 1938), and *Studies in Milton* (London, 1951). To these was belatedly added a pamphlet on dead issues: *The Metaphysicals and Milton* (London, 1956). C. S. Lewis' *A Preface to Paradise Lost* (London, 1942) and A. J. A. Waldock's *Paradise Lost and its Critics* (Cambridge, 1947) both made a controversial impact, but are much the same impressionistic and psychologizing apologetics as that which characterizes Tillyard's books. Better in some sections than either was B. Rajan's *Paradise Lost and the Seventeenth Century Reader* (London, 1947), but the value of its remarks is dissipated by their being scattered in vast deserts of historical rehash or vague stylistic im- pressions.

[5] Arnold Stein, *Answerable Style: Essays on Paradise Lost* (Minneapolis, 1953); Don Cameron Allen, *The Harmonious Vision: Studies in Milton's Poetry* (Baltimore, 1954); W. B. C. Watkins, *An Anatomy of Milton's Verse* (Baton Rouge, 1955); Robert Martin Adams, *Ikon: John Milton and the Modern Critics* (Ithaca, 1955); Howard Schultz, *Milton and Forbidden Knowledge* (New York, 1955); Kester Svendsen, *Milton and Science* (Cam- bridge, Mass., 1956); Arnold Stein, *Heroic Knowledge: An Interpretation of Paradise Regained and Samson Agonistes* (Minneapolis, 1957); Rosemond Tuve, *Images and Themes in Five Poems by Milton* (Cambridge, Mass.,

It is not my intention in the following discussion to detract from the considerable and permanent values which modern critics have indubitably established as a part of our heritage from Donne and those poets regarded as his most sympathetic contemporaries. Rather, it is my gesture of faith to believe that poems choose their own critics. To extrapolate this thesis will lead me into speculation upon the meaning of the declined interest in Donne, a poet so accessible to the "explicator," and into association of the recent heightening of Milton's reputation with the rise of a critical mode which I rather reluctantly label "metaphoric."[6]

It will be seen in the course of what follows that, from one point of view, this descriptive term has been forced upon me by the usage of many of those practicing critics and aestheticians whose views and methods I set in contradistinction to the ways of the New Criticism. And it will be clear that I use the term as they use it, with an eye to the function rather than to the nature of metaphor: especially at those moments when tenor

---

1957); Isabel MacCaffrey, *Paradise Lost as "Myth"* (Cambridge, Mass., 1959); J. B. Broadbent, *Some Graver Subject: An Essay on Paradise Lost* (London, 1960); John Peter, *A Critique of Paradise Lost* (New York, 1960).

[6] The following essay implies my disagreement with recent attempts to explain the direction of contemporary criticism: see Roy Harvey Pearce, "Historicism Once More," *KR*, XX (1958), 554-91; Hyatt Waggoner, "The Current Revolt Against the New Criticism," *Criticism*, I (1959), 211-25; Duncan, *Revival of Metaphysical Poetry*, pp. 174-81. The most valuable examination of the modern main stream and its heritage I find in Frank Kermode, *Romantic Image* (New York, 1957). Kermode superbly analyzes the fulcrum of that critical seesaw which made Donne rise at Milton's expense under the pressure of a false history written in defense of a valuable Symbolist aesthetic. While he does not attempt to predict the "new categories and still unheard persuasions" which will dominate future criticism, Kermode's closing words might serve as epigraph for the shifting interest which I hope to explain: "The time cannot be far off when [*Paradise Lost*] will be read once more as the most perfect achievement of English poetry, perhaps the richest and most intricately beautiful poem in the world. . . . If poets turn back to Milton they will . . . discover, if I may use the lines eulogistically, 'mere' now meaning 'pure,' that 'He has found, after the manner of his kind, / Mere images'" (pp. 165-6).

and vehicle draw so closely together that language becomes an immediate structural clarification, rather than a signatory betrayal, of experience.

In the course of examining Heraclitus' place in the development of pre-Socratic philosophy, Philip Wheelwright has emphasized that just this inextricable drawing together of the two poles of a depth metaphor (as opposed to a grammatically telescoped and, hence, reversible simile) constituted Heraclitus' instrument for surpassing the monistic tendencies of the earlier naturalist and transcendentalist systems simultaneously, by uniting their truths: "the fire of which he speaks is neither strictly physical nor strictly metaphysical; it is physical and metaphysical together; for it is the feeding flame, perceptible both to outward sight and as inward exuberance, and at the same time it is the universal fact of perpetual change."[7] In the course of his analysis, Wheelwright observes that this metaphoric language in the fragments is precisely that element which earned for Heraclitus his sobriquet, The Dark One. Because the radical acceptance of metaphor involves one in "the ontological status of paradox— an acceptance, that is to say, of the view that paradox lies inextricably at the very heart of reality."[8]

In brief, metaphor which cannot be expanded into simile cannot be "unsaid," because, "by literal standards [it] says too much. We declare, 'Fire is divine,' or we turn the sentence around and declare, 'God is fire.' And the result, in either direction—if the implications of the transcendental term are not ignored or caricatured—is flagrantly paradoxical."[9] And radical paradox quite as clearly must be read with a mind aware of the metaphoric connotations encompassing its terms, if it is not to

[7] Philip Wheelwright, *Heraclitus* (Princeton, 1959), p. 93; cf. pp. 13-5, 91-101.
[8] Ibid., p. 92.
[9] Ibid., p. 97.

be read as sheer nonsense. Heraclitus' "the way up and the way down are one and the same"; Keats' "vast shade in midst of his own brightness"; and Milton's "darkness visible" do not convey meaning without the double awareness engendered by metaphor.

It will become clear as my analysis develops that I also choose the term "metaphoric" because I believe that *Paradise Lost* can best be understood as a poem in which certain repeated metaphors mimetically express the epic theme with an unprecedented tenacity. And I hope that my argument will be convincing evidence for assertions concerning the radical interdependence of metaphor and paradox. For I will attempt to demonstrate how Milton, through this peculiarly structural development of metaphors, resolved the dilemma of reconciling the paradoxical modes of Christian expression for individual religious experience with interpersonal communication. Before attempting the demonstration, however, I will turn to a survey of some of those historical pressures which were both intensifying the dilemma and promoting its solution in the seventeenth century — to the immediate background of what I consider to be the primary organization of *Paradise Lost*.

This wedding of Miltonic and modern aesthetic fulcrums is not casual. Let me make explicit at the outset what I suppose is implied throughout the following pages: I view these immediate pressures which shaped Milton's way of creating a poem as also the ultimate background against which we may understand contemporary critical categories, the seed ground of our own aesthetic focus. And to clarify this significant sense in which we may speak of Milton's "modernity," I must begin by examining the phenomenon itself, that "metaphoric" organization of experience which is now most characteristic of criticism. Put most simply, my argument is that (if I have properly described the common denominator) this school of criticism is historically determined as an instrument appropriate for revealing the values of Milton's poem.

IT IS A safe enough commonplace, I think, that the New Criticism, in spite of its later attempts to isolate a poetic object, had its roots in psychology. To verify the remark, we need only look in the direction of I. A. Richards' early studies of the aesthetic process, T. E. Hulme's ambivalent fascination with Bergson,[10] or the centrality of the genre of lyric in the explicatory canon. This psychological orientation was, of course, only one mirroring of the *temporal* face of modern philosophy. As early as 1927 Wyndham Lewis was already quixotically tilting at an impressive list of the makers of modern thought who suffer from "an intense preoccupation with *time* or 'duration' (the

[10] Hulme is a classic case of a critic whose career was cut short in mid-motion from psychologism toward the spatialization I later discuss. In the notes toward modern art he utilizes Worringer, the stimulus for Frank's thinking about the novel (see below, page 15); and in the notes for *Cinders* he records: "The idealists analyse space into a mode of arranging sensations. But this gives us an unimaginable world existing all at a point. Why not try the reverse process and put all ideas (purely mental states) into terms of *space*. . . . The sense of reality is inevitably connected with that of *space*" (*Speculations*, ed. Herbert Read [New York and London, 1924], p. 240). On Hulme's larger ambivalence toward the imagination, of which this statement is a corollary, see Murray Krieger, *The New Apologists for Poetry* (Minneapolis, 1956), pp. 31-45. The whole tenor of Krieger's study is to reveal the New Critics' attempts to incorporate Richards' contextualism, while escaping the implications of his psychologistic orientation and the problems it raised both for the function and the objective status of the poem. But see particularly the discussions on pp. 114-22, 123-39, 183-8. In the course of their tortuous development, critics such as Brooks and Eliot (particularly in "Tradition and the Individual Talent"), showed tendencies toward the "metaphoric" approach to literature as my discussion defines it. It never, however, became a dominant element in either theory or practice within this roughly similar group of contextualists. Perhaps Hulme's flirtation was the most serious manifestation. Cf. Kermode, *Romantic Image*, pp. 119-37, on Hulme's dilemma and (pp. 140-61) the "dissociation of sensibility" dogma which emerged from it in New Critics, English and American.

psychological aspect of time, that is)."[11] And Lewis was perceptive at least in sorting out Joyce from the shoal of epigoni who
now appear only in the fine print in historical footnotes; the
Irishman seemed to occupy the bad eminence at the peak of a
pernicious tradition: "Without all the uniform pervasive growth
of the time-philosophy starting from the little seed planted by
Bergson, discredited, and now spreading more vigorously than
ever, there would be no *Ulysses,* or there would be no *A la
Recherche du Temps perdu.* There would be no 'time-composi-
tion' of Miss Stein; no fugues in words. In short, Mr. Joyce is
very strictly of the school of Bergson-Einstein, Stein-Proust"
(p. 89).

And the wide interest in psychological states as they are
temporal processes was leading Joyce's admirer T. S. Eliot to
Metaphysical poetry. In Eliot's classic phrases, Donne or Marvell
have "a direct sensuous apprehension of thought. . . . they . . .
feel their thought as immediately as the odour of a rose." But
this apprehension is nonetheless developed temporally within
that objective correlative which is the poem, since the parts of
a Metaphysical lyric have, to again cite Eliot, "something like a
syllogistic relation to each other," "a development by rapid
association of thought which requires considerable agility on the
part of the reader."[12] The analysis of poem as process became
standard practice. Allen Tate found that "the development of
imagery by logical extension, the reasonable framework being an
Ariadne's thread that the poet will not permit us to lose, is
the hallmark of the poetry called metaphysical."[13] Doniphan

[11] *Time and Western Man* (1927; Boston, 1957), p. 111.

[12] My quotations are, respectively, from the reprints in T. S. Eliot, *Selected
Essays: 1917-1932* (New York, 1932), pp. 246-7, 254, 242. Duncan, *Revival
of Metaphysical Poetry,* pp. 144-9, however, traces Eliot's cycle through the
enthusiasm of the twenties, to certain reservations about the Metaphysicals
(in deference to Dante) in the thirties, and ultimately to the partial revaluation of Milton in 1948.

[13] "Tension in Poetry," in *On the Limits of Poetry* (New York, 1948),
p. 80.

Louthan concluded that "training in (or long acquaintance with) patristic methods of exegesis, inclined Donne towards dialectical style."[14] And Joan Bennett describes the Metaphysical poem as moving from "the contemplation of a fact to a deduction . . . to a conclusion."[15]

It will be noticed that all of these comments are concentrated upon the *method* of the poet, not upon the shape of the poem or the structure of its rationale. Indeed, only very recently has Cleanth Brooks' widely-known reading of Donne been challenged as an inversion of ends and means. "It is one thing," suggests William Rooney in a comment that might apply to many Metaphysical readings, "to say that a poem is *made of paradoxical meanings* and quite another thing to conclude that the poem *functions to convey* a paradox."[16] But it was quite natural to overemphasize method when discussing the Metaphysicals, because their poetry was composed under the influence of mechanical directions toward a process by which one might unite Eliot's "sensuous apprehension" to "thought."

In the book which I have described as marking the close of the Metaphysical revival, Martz fulfilled his aim of modifying "the view of literary history which sees a 'Donne tradition' in English religious poetry, . . . [suggesting] instead a 'meditative tradition.' "[17] Turning to the multitude of meditational handbooks of the Renaissance, wherein men were taught to unify memory, understanding, and will, the soul's three powers, around a divine point for contemplation, Martz found the structural origin of the "dialectical," "logical," and yet strangely personal

[14] *The Poetry of John Donne: A Study in Explication* (New York, 1951), p. 29.
[15] *Four Metaphysical Poets* (Cambridge, 1934), pp. 7-8. Cf. the critics cited in Duncan, *Revival of Metaphysical Poetry*, pp. 18-9, 123.
[16] William J. Rooney, " 'The Canonization'—The Language of Paradox Reconsidered," *ELH*, XXIII (1956), 46.
[17] Louis L. Martz, *The Poetry of Meditation* (New Haven, 1954), p. 3. Later Martz further attempted to read *Paradise Regained* as a meditative structure which followed meditational handbooks only loosely: *"Paradise Regained:* The Meditative Combat," *ELH*, XXVII (1960), 223-47.

poetry of the Metaphysical favorites. Having detailed the elaborate steps in Ignatius Loyola's "application of the senses," Martz concludes: "It staggers the mind to ponder the effect that such a complex sequence would have upon a poet. . . . It should produce a hitherto unparalleled integration of feeling and thought."[18] Now, the "sensuous" element derived from the initial step in Ignatian meditational procedures is that vivification of the memory called "composition of place." "We must see the place where the things we meditate on were wrought, by imagining ourselves to be really present at those places; which we must endeavour to represent so lively, as though we saw them indeed, with our corporall eyes." [19] At first thought, this might seem to represent a conquest of time, a step outside that durational cage from which Wyndham Lewis urged escape. In one sense, this supposition is accurate. Viewed in its doctrinal rationale, "composition of place" can become a technique for internalizing incarnational theory. We are made to appropriate to our own circumstances of self-examination a sense of the eternal presence of Christ. It is out of the exploration of this union between the historical and the perpetual incarnation that Donne creates the superimposition of historical myth upon personal microcosm in

> Spit in my face yee Jewes, and pierce my side,
> Buffet, and scoffe, scourge, and crucifie mee,
> For I have sinn'd, and sinn'd, and onely hee,
> Who could do no iniquitie, hath dyed:
> But by my death can not be satisfied
> My sinnes, which passe the Jewes impiety:
> They kill'd once an inglorious man, but I
> Crucifie him daily, being now glorified.[20]

[18] Ibid., p. 79.
[19] Richard Gibbons, quoted in Martz, p. 27.
[20] John Donne, *The Divine Poems*, ed. Helen Gardner (Oxford, 1952), p. 9.

The same fusion is obtained in the "Nativity" sonnet for Magdalen Herbert in which we are confronted with a direct composition of place "in this stall" which is yet taken outside of history as the poet turns to query, "Seest thou, my Soule, with thy faiths eyes, how he / . . . doth lye," and which returns to a fused time prophetic of Milton's "Nativity Ode" when the poet instructs his soul: "Kisse him, and with him into Egypt goe, / *With his kinde mother, who partakes thy woe.*"[21]

But the central force of the meditational tradition was not effective in directing poetry into this atemporal channel, a mode having natural affinities with the efforts of our own time to juxtapose myths — efforts which will be cited in the course of this discussion. Rather, one finds upon broader exploration that the conformity of poetic to meditational pattern appears less often and less successfully within a single divine poem than within the structure of developmentally linked series, such as Donne's "La Corona," Herbert's *Temple* or Traherne's poetic manuscripts.[22] And in such cases, the sense of mystic union between the historic myth and its eternal presentness is dissipated, as the corporal act of the past becomes mere history, existing in the temporal associations of a memory which conjures up the scene as stimulus for the intellectual and affective commentary of the present. In short, despite its intentional origins, the act of meditation ultimately encourages a structure of processive rather than superimposed relationships.

This effect of the technique can be emphasized further by reviewing Donne's achievement from a somewhat different vantage point. If we attend to the secular rather than to the divine poems, we discover that it is here that Donne consistently composes scenic frameworks represented "so lively, as though we saw them indeed, with our corporall eyes." And not only do the

---

[21] Ibid., p. 3.
[22] See Martz, *Poetry of Meditation*, pp. 107-12, 288-320; John Malcolm Wallace, "Thomas Traherne and the Structure of Meditation," *ELH*, XXV (1958), 79-89.

secular poems develop internally with "something like a syllogistic relation," but repeatedly the sun plays a major part in the
scenic structure as both evidence and measure of the desperate
temporality of events.[23] Indeed, if time has seemed for one great
tradition only the shadow of eternity, Donne inverts the formula
in order to consume the fountain in the stream: "The Sun
itself, which makes times, as they pass, / Is elder by a year,
now."[24]

It is just this dominantly processive, temporal orientation of
Metaphysical-become-meditational poetry which accounts for
its abandonment by a large part of the serious critical audience in
favor of Milton, a point I hope to clarify in the following pages.[25]

Significantly, in *Finnegans Wake* Joyce replied to Wyndham
Lewis' strictures by parodying *Time and Western Man* as *Spice
and Westend Woman* because the *Wake* is a poem of which
memory is the subject, but a great circle of infinite recurrences
is the primarily spatial form. It was Joyce's manner of affirming
what the mathematician, Hermann Minkowski, formulated as a
postulate fifty years ago: "Henceforth space by itself, and time
by itself, are doomed to fade away into mere shadows, and only
a kind of union of the two will preserve an independent reality."[26]
It may be observed in passing that the Lewisite view is still

[23] Cf. "The Sun Rising," "Sweetest love, I do not go for weariness of
thee," "Break of Day," "The Anniversary," "The Dream," "A Nocturnal
upon St. Lucy's Day," "The Blossom," "A Lecture upon the Shadow."

[24] "The Anniversary," lines 3-4.

[25] Martz himself has failed to analyze the complex modern attitude toward
temporal structures, and therefore in his own way perpetuates the association
of Donne with modern poetry by way of meditational discipline: see pp. 321-
30, and a more recent restatement in "Donne and the Meditative Tradition,"
Thought, XXXIV (1959), 269-78. In the later article he is most insistent
upon the centrality of an "act of finding" (p. 277), a "process by which
unity of mind is discovered" (p. 272). He is, however, prompted to write by
an awareness that, in spite of his thesis, there has been a growing reaction
against Donne's reputation in favor of, among others, Milton.

[26] *Space and Time* as quoted in Sigfried Giedion, *Space, Time and Architecture* (3rd ed.; Cambridge, Mass., 1954), p. 14. Joyce's "spatial" structure
has been discussed in many places. For a convenient cross section, see William
Troy, "Notes on *Finnegans Wake*" (1939); Frank Budgen, "Joyce's Chapters
of Going Forth by Day" (1941); Frederick J. Hoffman, "Infroyce" (1945);

vigorous, as evidenced by the very recent analysis in which Lawrence Durrell set his own Alexandrian tetralogy against Joyce's technique:

> Modern literature offers us no Unities, so I have turned to science and am trying to complete a four-decker novel whose form is based on the relativity proposition. . . .
> The three first parts . . . are to be deployed spatially . . . and are not linked in a serial form. They interlap, interweave, in a purely spatial relation. Time is stayed. . . .
> This is not Proustian or Joycean method—for they illustrate Bergsonian "Duration" in my opinion, not "Space-Time."[27]

Clearly, in developing an already venerable history, the concept of space-time has not lapsed into the casualness usually accorded a commonplace. Rather, its cultural and philosophical implications have continued to excite exploratory efforts from investigators of widely varying persuasions and viewpoints. The most extensive impact, of course, has come from the incalculably influential work of Ernst Cassirer, whose *Philosophy of Symbolic Forms* constitutes the *Grundlage* for later popular studies in the vein of his own *Myth and Language* and Susanne Langer's *Philosophy in a New Key*.[28]

---

and Stuart Gilbert, "James Joyce" (1946)—all reprinted in *James Joyce: Two Decades of Criticism,* ed. Seon Givens (New York, 1948), pp. 309, 312-3, 317, 348, 416, 429, 453-4. Samuel Beckett, earliest commentator upon Joyce's space-time structuring, crossed it with Proustian qualities in his own bilingual novels: see Melvin J. Friedman, "The Novels of Samuel Beckett: An Amalgam of Joyce and Proust," *CL,* XII (1960), 47-58, esp. 48, 53-4. It is noteworthy that Giedion, discussed below, was a close associate of Joyce in the Zurich years; see Richard Ellmann, *James Joyce* (New York, 1959), pp. 635 ff., 749 ff., *et passim,* and Carola Giedion-Welcker *et al., In Memoriam: James Joyce* (Zurich, 1941).

[27] "Note" prefatory to *Balthazar* (New York, 1958); cf. *Mountolive* (New York, 1959), p. 285; *Clea* (New York, 1960), pp. 12-4, 135-6, 143. It will become apparent that I am not of Durrell's opinion; Joyce's structures are spatially more complex than Durrell's internovel relations.

[28] For our present purposes, two observations are worth making without pretending to trace the development of Cassirer's thought. The first is that

For the student of aesthetic form, however, two studies have been of even more particular significance. The first of these is Sigfried Giedion's *Space, Time and Architecture,* which appeared in 1941. Trained under Heinrich Wölfflin, who was the pupil of Jakob Burckhardt, Giedion brought to bear upon modern culture the same synthesizing techniques which his teachers had applied to the Renaissance. His achievement was to document the shift from three-dimensional perspective, finally abandoned by the Cubists early in this century, toward a new conception of planes in both painting and architecture, a conception that adapted the plane to the context of its civilization:

> Cubism breaks with . . . perspective. It views objects relatively: that is, from several points of view, no one of which has exclusive authority. And in so dissecting objects it sees them simultaneously from all sides. . . . It goes around and into its objects. Thus, to the three dimensions . . . which have held good . . . throughout so many centuries, there is added a fourth one—time. . . . The presentation of objects from several points of view introduces a new principle which is intimately bound up with modern life—simultaneity.[29]

The flow of time which has its literary reflection in the Aristotelian development of an action having beginning, middle, and end is here being frozen into the labyrinthine planes of a spatial block which, like the immense organization of Rockefeller

---

his creative theories of language and myth emerged gradually through a study of symbolic form in the Renaissance: I would mark *Individuum und Kosmos in der Philosophie der Renaissance* (1927) as the pivotal monograph. The second point is that Cassirer deals extensively with the dimensions of mythic space-time in ways implicitly pertinent to much of the following discussion in *The Philosophy of Symbolic Forms,* tr. Ralph Mannheim (New Haven, 1953-7), II, 44-6, 83-151, *et passim.* The depth to which the space-time dimension has permeated modern conceptualization has been surveyed in the work of G. Matoré; see "Le Vocabulaire Contemporain et L'Espace," *Revue des Sciences Humaines,* n.s., fasc. 97 (1960), 105-24.

[29] *Space, Time and Architecture,* p. 432.

Center,[30] can only be perceived by traveling both temporally and physically from point to point, but whose form has neither beginning, middle, end, nor center, and must be effectively conceived as a simultaneity of multiple views.

The other study in the aesthetics of space-time which I find highly significant is Joseph Frank's "Spatial Form in Modern Literature," first published in 1945.[31] Frank, too, found inspiration in the history of the plastic arts, emphasizing that naturalistic depth perspective gives objects a "time-value because it connects them with the real world in which events occur." On the other hand, "when depth disappears and objects are presented in one plane, their simultaneous apprehension as part of a timeless unity is obviously made easier."[32] An analogous substitution has been made in the work of Pound, Eliot or Joyce, who

> all deal, in one way or another, with the clash of historical perspectives induced by the identification of contemporary figures and events with various historical prototypes. . . . By this juxtaposition of past and present . . . history becomes unhistorical. . . . The objective historical imagination, . . . is transformed by these writers into the mythical imagination for which historical time does not exist—the imagination that sees the actions and events of a particular time merely as the bodying forth of eternal prototypes. These prototypes are created by transmuting the time-world of history into the timeless world of myth. And it is this timeless world of myth, forming the common content of modern literature, which finds its appropriate aesthetic expression in spatial form,

that is, "the reader is intended to apprehend their work spatially, in a moment of time, rather than as a sequence."[33]

Now, by the concept of "myth" I believe most modern com-

---

[30] Cf. ibid., pp. 744-55.
[31] *The Sewanee Review*, LIII (1945), 221-40, 433-56, 643-53. A revised version was published in *Criticism: The Foundations of Modern Literary Judgment*, ed. Mark Shorer, Josephine Miles, and Gordon McKenzie (New York, 1948), pp. 379-92.
[32] *Criticism*, p. 391.
[33] Ibid., pp. 392, 381.

mentators to understand man's practice of becoming the symbol of his own spiritual experience through projection of inner states into certain recurring narrative and scenic images. So understood, myth functions as a species of extended metaphor. It is as a consequence of this relationship, I think, that we find "myth" occupying a central position in Northrop Frye's *Anatomy of Criticism,* a book which already has received wide, if not uncritical, recognition as the twentieth century's richest contribution to aesthetic theory. The critic's *Finnegans Wake,* this study is a great circular organization of mutating categories which attempts to "place" all written phenomena in their familial relationships. In Frye's work, we again recognize an aesthetic created for a space-time cosmos: "Recurrence," observes Frye, "is usually spoken of as rhythm when it moves along in time, and as pattern when it is spread out in space. . . . The score of a symphony may be studied all at once, as a spread-out pattern: a painting may be studied as the track of an intricate dance of the eye. Works of literature also move in time like music and spread out in images like painting."[34] Further, the two modes of form are organic derivatives of Frye's conception of the role of criticism. For he sees the ultimately highest modes of literature as being mythic, rather than mimetic, i.e., creative rather than imitative of nature. And the linguistic analogue is the metaphor, as opposed to the discursive "sigmatic . . . verbal replica of external phenomena": "whatever is constructive in any verbal structure seems to me to be invariably some kind of metaphor or hypothetical identification . . . metaphors in their turn become the units of the myth or constructive principle of the argument."[35]

Therefore, he suggests that literature has functioned like mathematics in imposing mythic form upon the universe: "Mathematics is at first a form of understanding an objective

[34] Northrop Frye, *Anatomy of Criticism* (Princeton, 1957), p. 77.
[35] Ibid., p. 353.

world regarded as its content, but in the end it conceives of the content as being itself mathematical in form, and when a conception of a mathematical universe is reached, form and content become the same thing."[36] But the pattern of literature has *its* total metaphor in the conception of nature it has created as its image. Hence, Frye's organization of modes, phases, and genres is developed in circular scales bearing relation to the four "phases" of myth: comedy, romance, tragedy, and satire; these themselves are imaged in their relations to one another by metaphoric seasons: spring, summer, autumn, and winter.

I will not pretend to do more than suggest the logical skeleton of Frye's rationale for a terminology which at first meeting appears apocalyptic. But the point, for our purposes, is that in his *Anatomy of Criticism* the conception that the metaphor is the creative monad of the linguistic process leads into an elaborate architecture of interrelated points on dialectical circles; and yet, the ground metaphor for the entire structure is temporal: the seasons. Metaphor projects itself into the flux which is nature, creates a sense of process from that flux, and then borrows this process image back, but now in the spatial form of the circle which corresponds to the temporal image of cyclical motion. Time-space in this instance becomes not an aesthetic insight but a system of aesthetics—yet the form of its expression is like that found by Frank in the modern mythologists: time is the subject matter which paradoxically ends as spatial pattern.

Less dramatically, another influential theoretician has suggested the space-time dimension in elaborating the term "verbal icon" to describe the literary object. William Wimsatt has developed a large share of his thinking in response to felt inadequacies of the rather militant Neo-Aristotelians at the University of Chicago, for whom the temporal line of plot has seemed primary as a feature not only of the narrative but of the lyric genre. And in responding, Wimsatt found it necessary, not so

[36] Ibid., p. 352.

much to set the metaphoric against the mimetic, as to exhibit how the poetic object engulfs mimetic process in stable form. In a key statement, he insists that "there are no poems which are in some exclusively proper way 'mimetic' and which hence should not be permitted a symbolic reading; and conversely, all 'symbolic' poems, if they are real poems, are in some important sense 'mimetic' and dramatic. . . . I believe — in direct contradiction . . . of Chicago doctrine — that analogy and metaphor are not only in a broad sense the principle of all poetry but are also inevitable in practical criticism."[37]

Giedion and Frank find time being spatialized in the creative artists around them; Frye and Wimsatt make this union the substructure of an aesthetic for moderns. Other scholar-critics are finding the same process at work in that most obviously temporal of verbal forms, the drama. G. Wilson Knight in 1930 thus prefaced his finest book with a challenge to orthodoxy:

> To receive the . . . Shakespearian vision . . . One must be prepared to see the whole play in space as well as in time. It is natural . . . to pursue the steps of the tale in sequence, . . . regarding those essentials that Aristotle noted: the beginning, middle, and end. But by giving supreme attention to this temporal nature of drama we omit what, in Shakespeare, is at least of equivalent importance. A Shakespearian tragedy is set spatially as well as temporally in the mind. . . . there are throughout the play a set of correspondences which relate to each other independently of the time-sequence which is the story.[38]

Knight's own practice opened the way for a deluge of Shakespearean imagery studies in the forties, the most extreme of

[37] *The Verbal Icon: Studies in the Meaning of Poetry* (1954; New York, 1958), p. 49. Wimsatt's definition and fullest technical discussion of metaphor appears on pp. 119-30, esp. 127-30.

[38] *The Wheel of Fire* (1930; 4th ed., rev. and enlarged; London, 1949), p. 3.

which was Robert Heilman's *This Great Stage,* an interpretation of *King Lear.* In Heilman's statement of presuppositions, it
is interesting to notice that not only the theory, but the language
in which it is phrased, has been permeated by the conception
of literature as a space-time solid in which we can connect
disparate temporal points as if they were areas in a crystalline
verbal cube: "a series of dramatic statments about one subject
does constitute a bloc of meaning which is a structural part
of the play. This bloc may be understood as one of the author's
metaphors. It is a metaphor just as a body of recurrent images,
with its burden of implications, is a metaphor. The dramatist's
basic metaphor is his plot. . . . All the constituent metaphors
must be related to the large metaphor which is the play itself."[39]

Maynard Mack, a less explicit critic, proceeds along the same
lines in a recent essay titled "The World of Hamlet." The
mode by which Mack reveals the coherence of this world is
simply to weave into associational patterns the radical metaphors
of the dramatic dialogue until he has prepared a reading which
halts the literal movement of plot action at the close of *Hamlet*
by freezing it into the stasis of metaphor. "We know that Hamlet
is ready for the final contest of mighty opposites. He accepts
the world as it is, the world as a duel, in which, whether we
know it or not, evil holds the poisoned rapier and the poisoned
chalice waits; and in which, if we win at all, it costs no less
than everything."[40] Verbal metaphors have transmuted plot into
a metaphor for Hamlet's state of mind, which itself is a metaphor for the human predicament.

I do not wish to leave the impression that I agree whole-
heartedly with the particular views of any of these critics, nor

---

[39] *This Great Stage: Image and Structure in King Lear* (Baton Rouge,
1948), pp. 11-2. Cf. Heilman's later study, *Magic in the Web: Action and
Language in Othello* (Lexington, 1956).
[40] "The World of Hamlet," reprinted from *The Yale Review* (1952), in
Shakespeare: Modern Essays in Criticism, ed. Leonard Dean (New York,
1957), p. 257.

do I mean to suggest that they are unique. Quite the reverse. I wish only to give some indication of how thoroughly the reaction against a temporal preoccupation has influenced both practical criticism and aesthetic theory. In its place there has arisen a more complex orientation which attempts to utilize the metaphor as the monadic component of the mind's formal marriage of time with space. I hope to have suggested why the New Critics' characteristically developmental technique of *explication de textes*, has come to seem anachronistic in the wake of a criticism no less dedicated to verbal analysis. And when the interest of critics shifted toward this new mode, it was inevitable that they should abandon as the focus of taste the "Metaphysical" poets who had exerted such a fascination for proponents of a critical technique that was, as were the poems, temporal in structure. Now I should like to ask how and why the contemporary critic reads Milton.

While I elect to examine the work of only three among the readers of Milton catalogued earlier, it is to be understood that the others, with varying degrees of eclecticism and perception, have made similar approaches to the poems, although without such urgent and articulate commitment to a method.

Probably Francis Fergusson was moved in reaction to the literalism of the Chicago School to reinterpret Aristotle, so that the Greek's idea of "action" becomes the center for an "Idea of a Theater,"[41] And "action" (*praxis*), writes Fergusson, "does not

---

[41] Paradoxically, while drama studies (Fergusson, Heilman, Mack, Knight, Bethell, Traversi) have been developing in a direction which moves away from the traditional conception of plot-as-imitation based upon the reading of Aristotle as a naturalistic critic, nondramatic studies, at the same time, have often been introducing dramatic development as a basic criterion of literary structures. I illustrate this in respect of Milton in my examination of Arnold Stein's readings below; one finds similar tendencies in the treatment of *Paradise Regained* in Don Cameron Allen, *The Harmonious Vision*, pp. 112, 118, 120, *et passim*.

Such an unexpected development seems to me to result from the rise of Chicago Neo-Aristotelianism, that movement in which the new academic criticism found an important stimulus after R. S. Crane's notable conversion.

mean outward deeds or events, but something much more like 'purpose' or 'aim'. . . . the plot of a play is the arrangement of outward deeds or incidents, and the dramatist uses it, as Aristotle tells us, as the first means of imitating the action."[42] Arnold Stein, borrowing the phrase "drama of [the] mind"[43] from Fergusson, has also imported his theory of "action" (which is another transmutation of "plot" into a metaphor for "end") for a reading of Milton's three major poems.

It is not surprising that a critic who served his apprenticeship as a reader of Donne should be inclined to hear the developing dialectic of drama in twin epics. But it is revelatory of the temper of recent years that he should attempt to utilize this drama as an instrument for establishing the presence of "myth." Toward the close of his book on *Paradise Lost*, Stein asserts that "Definition is determined by dramatic trial; rising toward God can be expressed only by myth, but false myth can be distinguished from true only by dramatic definition."[44] The "drama," then, is the limited voice of each character, expressing in ideational and active terms his limited understanding of "this great argument"; the "myth" is the poem which expresses the argument: "[*Paradise Lost*] has the form of drama. . . .

Those who have taken their cues from the Chicagoans appear not to have grasped the implications of what the dramatic critics have sensed and what Father Ong (see below) has documented: that Aristotle formulated a poetic for an aural rather than a visual age of communication, and that to force the limitations of the former upon the literature of the latter is to sacrifice the modern potentiality for simultaneity of perception. See Krieger, *New Apologists for Poetry*, pp. 95-6, 150-4, 195-6, for a pertinent analysis of the Chicagoans' quarrel with critics other than Wimsatt.

[42] Francis Fergusson, *The Human Image in Dramatic Literature* (Garden City, 1957), pp. 115-6 (the essay was first published in 1952). Cf. *The Idea of a Theater* (1949; Garden City, 1953), pp. 242-55.

[43] *Heroic Knowledge* (Minneapolis, 1957), p. 96. Cf. the insistence upon the "dramatic" structure of *Paradise Lost* in *Answerable Style*, pp. 4, 14-5, 46, 50, 58-9, 93, 95, 116-8, 123 (this last a crucial defining passage, but not altogether inclusive in its definitions of the definitions of "drama" implied in Stein's text). I have reviewed *Heroic Knowledge* at more length in *JAAC*, XVII (1959), 402-3.

[44] *Answerable Style*, p. 116.

Within that form definition continuously purifies, but what it purifies continuously passes beyond dramatic definition into the great and central mythic vision."[45] The explanation is finally arrived at through a statement on Milton's perception: Stein acknowledges that there may seem a certain perverseness in applying "dramatic" as a defining label for *Paradise Lost,* but insists that Milton "as a man . . . saw the most significant human experience and human destiny itself as a kind of drama."[46]

In sum, Stein reads the epic as a drama of mind, but since the process of mind is mythic, the poem ultimately becomes a myth which employs drama as its radical metaphor. Stein's conclusion to his later reading of *Paradise Regained* is cautiously similar: "Milton nowhere insists on the literal identification of the reader with the hero; the tension of that relationship is maintained throughout the poem; it is for every man's conscience to assess the symbolism."[47] But if the case for the mythic end to which the drama is means in *Paradise Lost* does not seem totally convincing, it was at least argued. It is notable that we do not receive the symbolic reading of *Paradise Regained* as argument, but as epilogue: the passage I have cited occurs in the final paragraph of Stein's long analysis. Further, in a note appended to a summary of the four stages of Christ's spiritual development, Stein asserts: "What I have tried to express is a symbolism which is less historical than psychological, perhaps mythic."[48] This is clearly an attempt to unite the "drama" and the "myth" which were earlier separated, but revealingly the myth has become only "perhaps mythic."

Ultimately Stein is a Bradleyan essayist in psychology, translating "for the modern reader the moral issues into what I hope are their still-recognizable forms" (p. 217). And since, as the

[45] Ibid., p. 117.
[46] Ibid., p. 123.
[47] *Heroic Knowledge*, p. 134.
[48] Ibid., p. 223; cf. pp. 104-5.

notes frequently indicate, the critic's ethic has been influenced
by Bergson and Buber, the translation naturally falls into the
developmental rhythm of drama.[49] Further, "In drama, the stream
of motivation, once recognized above ground, following its
natural course, allows us to believe in the existence of a real
spring. We may speculate, legitimately and profitably, on what is
below ground" (p. 60). But to take this last step, of course,
is to abandon all pretense to conceive of the poem as "myth," or
"metaphor" or even "object." It is to return it, rather, to the
dynamic, but, therefore, shapeless, process of life. And yet, the
contemporary revaluation of metaphor and myth induced even
this self-conscious critic to misread his own aims, to believe that
he was revealing static form in a temporal movement.

Rosemond Tuve is truer to both Milton's poetic and the contemporary temper in her reading of some early lyrics and the
masque Comus as complex metaphors; in short, we again find
the apparent flow of drama being reinterpreted as a spatial object
in which temporally separate points must be simultaneously perceived. Of Comus she writes: "The whole myth had already become figurative, and in it chastity even as literal continence is a
type of something, shadows forth meanings as they operate in
another order";[50] Lycidas "is grounded in metaphor. It is figurative speech from first to last" (p. 86). And at the close of her
study she is explaining not only Comus but Milton when she
writes in phrases reminiscent of Heilman on Lear: "allegory is
not any series of little metaphors; it contains many such within
a metaphor, which is continued" (p. 159). The readings which
emerge from these premises are never extrapolations. They do
not, as Stein's do, pour extrinsic worlds into the poem, but
rather give shape (which, in such a metaphoric theory, is also
meaning) to the world in the poem's image.

And fine success in illuminating Paradise Lost was achieved

---

[49] Cf. ibid., p. 226, n. 13; p. 227 n. 3.
[50] Images and Themes in Five Poems by Milton, p. 138.

recently in Isabel McCaffrey's mythic analysis. More carefully than any previous reader, she has examined the working of the similes, the scenic areas, the imagery and discursive dialogue, to support conclusions which will by now sound familiar to my reader: "the geography of *Paradise Lost* provides a medium in which motion can take place without the awareness of temporal process — duration — that usually accompanies it" (p. 51); "this ability to apprehend time as a completed pattern gives it immediately a spatial quality; past and future become not periods, but places" (p. 53); "Milton experienced the world of his epic architecturally, in terms of mass and space. The modulation of time into spatial effects" was the result (pp. 76-7).

It might seem paradoxical to rank this critic with the "metaphorical" group, since she explicitly establishes a distinction: "metaphorical . . . styles in which meaning is enacted or adumbrated by analogous incidents and symbols, are . . . inappropriate for a poem which finds its subject in myth" (p. 38); and this, because in a "true" mythic poem the author believes the myth which, "far from being a symbolic version of some distant truth, is itself the model of which everyday reality is in some sense the symbol" (p. 16). But the significance of these statements is revealed by her later observation that when Milton "used metaphor and simile, the vehicle could almost without warning shift and become the tenor" (p. 108). For, actually, MacCaffrey's readings are "metaphoric" in that they consider the physical elements of the poem — light, dark, heights and depths — as themselves the affective articulation of the myth, rather than the backdrop of a theological poem. Indeed, this critic is the most truly "metaphorical" reader among Milton's admirers. But her difficulty in accepting the term arises from her implicit understanding of its weight; metaphor does not function as analogy. Its purpose, rather, is the conquest of temporal limitation, as is that of myth, if we understand the latter term as it has been defined in my earlier discussion.

In substantiating what is possibly a commonplace for a large body of current readers of poetry, who take for granted the symbolic form theories of Cassirer, one might be justified in simply recalling the influence from two decades of intensive public reading by Empson. But the most suggestive succinct statement on the function of metaphor with which I am familiar has been made by Sigurd Burckhardt. This critic reminds us that metaphor, the epitome of the poetic process itself, must effect a destructive action prior to its creative function. Because, argues Burckhardt, words are signs for things, the poet works in a medium which is debased by its removal from primary reference, a medium crucially different from paint, stone or musical chords with their existential immediacy. The poet's effort, therefore, is to unchain words from "their bondage to meaning, their purely referential role, and . . . give or restore to them the corporeality which a true medium needs."[51] And it is precisely in metaphor that words not only break the distortions of discursive syntax which imply a nonexperiential "process," but outrage and belie the insidious simplicity of perception which infects our ordinary use of language as a system of "signs." The inference is clear: "Metaphors, then, like puns and rhymes, corporealize language, because any device which interposes itself between words and their supposedly simple meanings calls attention to the words as things" (p. 283).

It is my conviction that just here, in their varying degrees of

[51] Sigurd Burckhardt, "The Poet as Fool and Priest," ELH, XXIII (1956), 279-98; I quote from p. 280. Cf. the less elaborate but corroborative essay by Walter J. Ong, "Metaphor and the Twinned Vision," SR, LXIII (1955), 193-201. Francis Ponge and other French critics have been equally engaged with this conception: see J. Robert Loy, "Things in Recent French Literature," PMLA, LXXI (1956), 27-41, esp. 36-7. Krieger, New Apologists for Poetry, pp. 73-5, 128-32, warns of the communicative limits of such theory while supporting its pragmatic usefulness. The Chicago Neo-Aristotelians' attacks on the more naïve formulations of metaphoric operation are valid only against critiques which attempt to define the poem-as-object rather than the "poetic" mode. The separation of the two can also raise impasses we need not worry here (see Krieger, pp. 93-8, 197).

conscious recognition of this central truth about poetry's way of life, we find cause for the fascination in which metaphoric reading holds contemporary critics, nurtured in a culture which so persistently subsumes time in a spatialized vision of reality. Time is the destroyer; for some decades, perhaps in the wake of that happy progressivism which emerged as an organic and evolutionary theory of life, we gratified that great antagonist by giving him hold upon our imagination. But we can now perceive that fascination with temporal process as a rip tide across the grander movement of man into the world of vast spaces which he projects from within to envelop and still the turning axle of a never-present *now*. And if Milton, as the following analyses will attempt to confirm, is a poet of all others most abundantly responsive to this imaginative process, we can understand why he should have been so garlanded with attention in recent years, understand that in the end of all it is Milton, not Donne, who is the poet for our time, who speaks in our idiom.

II

RAMISTIC
IMPLICATIONS

IF WHAT I HAVE SAID is convincing rather than
merely reflexively defensive, there is, as I earlier suggested,
more than accidental scholarly interest to account for my prefacing these readings in Milton with a discussion of contemporary
critical preoccupations. I propose, then, some further historical
inferences before turning from the question of why Milton's
epic structure became what it did to address myself to critical
definition of that structure.

For two decades Renaissance studies have been swept by con-
fusing crosscurrents from those engaged in delineating the relevance of Ramism for seventeenth-century modes of thought; and
nowhere has this interest been more vigorous than among historians of English and American literature. Of particular note
in our context is the implicit conflict between those who closely
interlace the rise of Metaphysical poetry with Ramistic logic and
those who view this logic as a primal organizing factor both in
the structure of Puritan thinking and in that of *Paradise Lost*.[1]

---

[1] To complicate issues further, defenders of each of these positions have
been openly attacked by others who deny the relevance of Ramism altogether

Rosemond Tuve's now-classic *Elizabethan and Metaphysical Imagery* proposed overlapping theses. First, that there is a continuing tradition of logically functioning imagery in the "English poetic tradition . . . of a piece from Marlowe (or Wyatt) to Marvell,"[2] that the felt difference in Metaphysical poetry results from the images being "more numerous, more consistently of one kind, and (this is the same point as the last) used for a narrower variety of functions."[3] Second, that the increasing popularity in the seventeenth century of the Ramistic reordering of the relations between logic and rhetoric accounts for this shift. The Ramistic insistence upon the axiomatic nature of individual terms or things which in themselves constitute "arguments" insofar as they have a "relatable*ness*,"[4] led, argues Tuve, in the Metaphysicals, to a "great stress on the capacity of 'specials' to *state* 'generals'. . . an emphasis upon the power of an image to convey a concept, the power of a particular to 'say' or make manifest a universal."[5] With some caution, she concludes: "I do not suggest that Ramistic attitudes produce none other than Metaphysical poems, but only that in an intellectual world where such attitudes toward imaginative literature became

---

at these points. For negative voices concerning the influence upon the Metaphysicals, see Joseph A. Mazzeo, "A Critique of Some Modern Theories of Metaphysical Poetry," *MP*, L (1952), 88-96, esp. 89-90; A. J. Smith, "An Examination of Some Claims Made for Ramism," *RES*, VII (1956), 348-59; George Watson, "Ramus, Miss Tuve, and the New Petromachia," *MP*, LV (1958), 259-62. Watson earlier implied that Ramism was an anti-Metaphysical influence indirectly through Hobbes: see "Hobbes and the Metaphysical Conceit," *JHI*, XVI (1955), 558-62. For denials of the importance of Ramism for an understanding of Milton see P. Albert Duhamel, "Milton's Alleged Ramism," *PMLA*, LXVII (1952), 1035-53, and John M. Steadman, " 'Man's First Disobedience': The Causal Structure of the Fall," *JHI*, XXII (1960), 180-97.

[2] *Elizabethan and Metaphysical Imagery* (Chicago, 1947), p. 351.

[3] Ibid., p. 343.

[4] On this crucial conception in Ramistic logic, see Tuve, pp. 334-53; Duhamel, "Milton's Alleged Ramism," pp. 1042-3; Ong (cited below), pp. 199-205.

[5] Ibid., p. 347.

every year more prevalent, no result is more natural than the dialectical toughness of the Metaphysical poem, its substitution of intellectual probing for rhetorical persuasion."[6]

But in a note contrasting Milton with Donne, Tuve explicitly exempts *Paradise Lost* from the tendency of which she is historian: "The most heightened style the Renaissance knew — the heroic — is not hospitable to images which function dialectically like those here considered, and luckily the greatest poet of the seventeenth century was not above suiting his style to the length of his poem. The slow *reader's pace* necessary in poems which emulate the acuteness of dialectic cannot but make us rejoice that Milton was too levelheaded to think that a follower of Ramus must toss out Mazzoni."[7]

George Watson commented with some wryness that "so far as the poets are concerned, there are only three who have . . . been shown to have been Ramists: Sidney, Ben Jonson, Milton. . . . while there is a deafening silence on the subject of Ramus on the part of Donne, Herbert, and Cowley."[8] And one can infer a similar misplacement of focus in Tuve's work from the retrospective vantage offered by Martz' study, which suggests a non-Ramistic and convincing source in the older meditational tradition for exactly the elements of Metaphysical style which Tuve traces to the impact of Ramism.

Surprisingly, in the course of her argument Tuve again and again pushed toward a conception of Renaissance poetic which seems much more obviously applicable to Milton and Bunyan than to Donne and Herbert. "This easy interchange between things and the meanings of things is subtly different from modern notions of the way images work. . . . One might phrase it carelessly and say that Elizabethans write and read images not like nominalists but like realists"; "Abstract notions of some

---

[6] Ibid., p. 343.
[7] Ibid., p. 372.
[8] "Ramus, Miss Tuve, and the New Petromachia," p. 261.

degree of profundity enter whenever the language is truly metaphorical, or whenever we can or must read the poem on a
figurative rather than a literal level. . . . Elizabethan readers
were more habituated to the . . . sort"; "Traditional ties between
logic and the poet's methods take on a new force against the background of the Ramist conception that *every* unit in *every* type of
discourse must, the moment it is seen in relation to any other
unit, inescapably make some minute step toward a true or false
disposition or pattern. Logic no longer merely offers the poet
helps; he cannot but take part in the universal and natural
attempt to trace out the reasonable pattern of reality."[9] These
passages clearly echo when, years later, Tuve turns to that reading of Milton's minor poems mentioned in the preceding chapter; but there we hear nothing of either Ramus or *Paradise
Lost.*

Perry Miller pioneered the serious analysis of the Ramistic
impact upon the Anglo-Saxon world in *The New England Mind:
The Seventeenth Century,* but seemed largely to miss its more
profound literary implications in his insistence upon structural
effects, especially in sermon literature (in which genre, however,
he argued that the effect was anti-Metaphysical).[10] It remained
for Charles Feidelson to explore more profoundly the ambiguities
involved in Puritan Ramism, although he too insisted upon invoking the Metaphysical conceit as a touchstone.

Briefly, Feidelson finds the Puritan mind at odds with itself.
On the one hand it is "radically metaphoric," so that past and
present coalesce, Anne Hutchinson becomes Sisera, Satan inhabits the Indians, and "the wearisome reiteration of 'provi-

---

[9] *Elizabethan and Metaphysical Imagery,* pp. 290, 156, 346.
[10] *The New England Mind: The Seventeenth Century* (Cambridge, Mass.,
1939), p. 345: "It was, obviously, impossible to be a Ramist and still preach
like John Donne." Tuve notes but refuses to argue the point (p. 424).
Miller's study was preceded by the discussion in Hardin Craig, *The En-
chanted Glass* (Oxford, 1936), pp. 140-59. Craig, however, saw Ramus merely
as a popularizer of a logic simple enough to supply a fashionable jargon for
poets and dramatists.

dences' in the Puritan writings is actually a record of symbolic experience that never attained formal literary structure."[11] What had happened, Feidelson finds, was the incompatible cross-breeding of the Puritans' providential conception "that united the objectivity of history with the meaningfulness of Scripture"[12] with the Ramistic reorientation toward the primacy of logic: "If the real structure of language and reality was purely logical, aesthetic form was merely an ornament . . . decoration added to and presupposing a logical framework." The result, when the Puritan turned to the world of felt symbols, was the logical "opening" of meanings, which usually merely "produced the bare bones of a metaphysical conceit, a paraphrase of a complex figure that never came into actual existence."[13] Here we are confronted, then, with a paradoxical antiphony to Tuve's reading of effects, in which Ramism *prevents* that very fruition of the Metaphysical mode which she had found it fostering.

Meanwhile, Leon Howard also had viewed the Ramistic impact upon Puritan literature from another standpoint altogether. He contended that if we looked into our Ramist logic we could find the structural principles of *Paradise Lost,* arguing that the Ramistic-Miltonic conception of causation was atemporal, and that *Paradise Lost* was precisely a poem dedicated to the causes of man's first disobedience and its fruits. Therefore, we must not seek a temporal structure in this poem of culminating causes — a processive "plot." Rather, we should recognize the poet's structural effort to be that of displaying "independent or parallel efficient causes which were not derived from some

---

[11] Charles Feidelson, Jr., *Symbolism and American Literature* (Chicago, 1953), p. 81.

[12] This conception of the divine "presentness" in contemporary history has been most satisfactorily explored for the Puritan consciousness, of course, in William Haller's *Liberty and Reformation in the Puritan Revolution* (New York, 1955), and "John Foxe and the Puritan Revolution" in R. F. Jones, et al., *The Seventeenth Century* (Stanford, 1951), pp. 209-24.

[13] *Symbolism and American Literature,* pp. 83-5.

'first cause' in any way perceptible to the human mind."[14] But this interesting explanation of argument and structure dissipated rapidly into a semantic quibble, as Howard abused the Ramistic emphasis upon convincing proof in relation to causation until he found himself maintaining that the development of Satan's character was intended for a piece of proof, and began to speak of "logical character."[15]

It remained for Father Walter J. Ong finally to clarify the Renaissance interest (and our own, if I infer correctly from the phenomena discussed in the first chapter of this book) in that shrouded figure, Peter Ramus, by preparing a study which not only explains the divergencies among the historical analyses we have reviewed here, but also forces us to reorient our understanding of late intellectual history in the West. The conclusion of his work can be simply stated: Ramism was the Renaissance manifestation in which Europe saw the Scholastic revolution completed, the revolution converting the ancient aural world into the spatial world of the printed book, into the mechanistic Newtonian universe, into a pattern of dichotomizing diagrams depicting the structure of every science from rhetoric to biography, into — in short — "method," as opposed to dialectic.[16] "Place" logic gradu-

---

[14] Leon Howard, " 'The Invention' of Milton's 'Great Argument': A Study of the Logic of God's Ways to Men," *HLQ*, IX (1946), 149-73 (I quote from p. 157).

[15] Ibid., pp. 159-60, *et passim*. A less coherent step in the same direction, although one which eschewed any actual application of logic to poem, was Thomas S. K. Scott-Craig's "The Craftsmanship and Theological Significance of Milton's *Art of Logic*," *HLQ*, XVII (1953), 1-16. Wilbur Samuel Howell, *Logic and Rhetoric in England, 1500-1700* (Princeton, 1956), pp. 211-9, reviews Milton's logic and seems indecisively to endorse Howard's view and to reject that of Duhamel. This wide-ranging study discusses Ramism at length, but raises few implications, and is largely irrelevant to the effect of Ramism upon Milton the poet insofar as it explicitly elects not "to give an account of the theories governing the production of Renaissance poetry, fiction, and drama" (p. v); it also fails to discuss the impact of shifting modes upon the practice of poetry.

[16] Walter J. Ong, *Ramus, Method, and the Decay of Dialogue* (Cambridge, Mass., 1958); *Ramus and Talon Inventory* (Cambridge, Mass., 1958). The argument of these books was anticipated in a number of earlier essays,

ally evolved into diagram, and it was the actual making physical of these dichotomies spawned of dichotomies which was the central aspect of the Ramist revolution of logic as it emerges from Ong's rich analysis. Unfortunately, it was this aspect of Ramism which Tuve had chosen explicitly to ignore in her treatment. "I make no attempt," she wrote, "to give a systematic review of Ramus' dialectic; this has been done, and many of the more important differences from peripatetic logic are impertinent to the concerns of this book. The famous 'dichotomies,' for example, I shall scarcely mention."[17] An unhappier misjudgment of proper emphases could scarcely have been made. In commenting upon Tuve's work, Ong observes that the intensified Renaissance concern with particulars is inextricable from the contemporary understanding of just these "dichotomies": "Ramist interest in 'specials' and its emphasis upon disjunction come to much the same thing. 'Specials' are thought of largely as 'generals' cut up into more or less quantitative pieces, and thus as a product of disjunction, effected in concepts more or less openly devised according to visual, spatial analogies."[18] And he proceeds to observe that this spatial orientation led Ramists in a direction diametrically opposite from the typical dialogue structure of the Metaphysical poem, adding that in fact "Ramists did not write metaphysical poetry, or, indeed, much poetry at all."

It is not in logic as a general entity, then, that we are to seek the aesthetic significance of Ramism, but in the particular spatialized form of logic which reduced reality to a visual object, and supplanted dialogue by the monologue of the expositor

---

the chief of which are: "Ramus, Rhetoric and the Pre-Newtonian Mind," in *English Institute Essays*, 1952 (New York, 1954), pp. 138-70; "Ramus and the Transit to the Modern Mind," *The Modern Schoolman*, XXXII (1955), 301-11; "System, Space, and Intellect in Renaissance Symbolism," *Bibliothèque d'Humanisme et Renaissance*, XVIII (1956), 222-39.

[17] Tuve, *Elizabethan and Metaphysical Imagery*, p. 332 n.
[18] *Ramus, Method, and the Decay of Dialogue*, p. 286.

pointing out the connections among parts. Once we understand this, we can perceive that Feidelson was quite right in discovering an antimetaphysical impact in Ramism; indeed, Ong concludes in a similar vein: "When the Puritan mentality, which is here the Ramist mentality, produces poetry, it is at first blatantly didactic, but shades gradually into reflective poetry which does not talk to anyone in particular but meditates upon objects."[19]

But antimetaphysical is not synonymous with antipoetic, a synonymity which Feidelson and Ong are too ready to permit us to infer. For, as Howard remarked, the greatest poet of the seventeenth century was also the Puritan author of a Ramistic logic. His poem is properly didactic. But it is didactic in a way which speaks to the whole of man. It is a spatial poem, as I have asserted and as I will argue; one might now say, with the historical vocabulary which Father Ong provides from the Renaissance, that it is a diagrammatic poem in which places cut across narrative to become interconnected into the image of this great argument, in which form emerges as continued metaphor. As such it is a poem which rises like a brilliant phoenix from the bitter ashes of the cruelest seventeenth-century dilemma.

Ramism was so protean that it could work in elusive and contradictory directions, and one direction its influence naturally took was not only antipoetic, but costly in the extreme to irenic yearnings to escape the impasse reached in the big wars and coils of religion which marked the Renaissance. As we have remarked, the poet's function is to release, primarily through metaphor, the referential hold of an outer "reality" upon those words with which he performs an impossible feat of creative prestidigitation by making them the world's body of a profounder reality. But in the Ramistic plan of dichotomies, laid out with emphasis upon visual relations, a plan which permits us to "see"

---

[19] Ibid., pp. 287-8.

the biography of Cicero at a single glance,[20] it is apparent that the referential bearing of words will have a natural emphasis.

Ramus had developed the habit of regarding everything, mental and physical, as composed of little corpuscular units of "simples." He never seems expressly aware of this habit, but it dominates all his thinking, subconsciously, yet stubbornly and absolutely. Ramus thus tends to view all intellectual operations as a spatial grouping of a number of these corpuscles into a kind of cluster, or as a breaking down of clusters into their corpuscular units. . . . having decided to call the groupings or clusters genera, Ramus proceeds adamantly to the conclusion that individuals and species are exactly the same thing. . . . the Ramist corpuscular epistemology, supposing that knowledge consists of sets of mental items, thereby implied one-for-one correspondence between terms and things.[21]

THIS INFLUENCE from the new logic flows into other traditions important to the Renaissance which reinforce the same point of view. We are familiar with Thomas Sprat's comment on the Royal Society's aims for philosophic discourse, published, like *Paradise Lost,* in 1667: "They have . . . a constant Resolution . . . to return back to the primitive purity, and shortness, when men deliver'd so many *things,* almost in an equal number of words."[22] Hobbes had earlier warned, "a man that seeketh precise *truth,* had need to remember what every name he uses stands for; and to place it accordingly";[23] John Hall "perceived that it was better to grave *things* in the mindes of children, then

---

[20] Cf. ibid., pp. 30-1, where Freige's biographical table is reproduced.
[21] Ibid., p. 202.
[22] Thomas Sprat, *The History of the Royal Society of London* (London, 1667), p. 113.
[23] *Leviathan;* ed. A. R. Waller (Cambridge, 1905), p. 17.

words";[24] while Abraham Cowley, more modestly, proposed a school where boys will be "initiated into Things as well as Words."[25] Contemporary versions of the dichotomy might be multiplied over many pages, but they represent simply the flowering (undoubtedly in great part owing to the mercurial rise of experimental method in the natural sciences) of an ancient tradition.[26] For it was Cato who advised, "Rem tene, verba sequentur," advice which echoed in both Cicero and Seneca, those master voices of the past for Renaissance readers.[27] This combination of old and new attitudes, of Ramistic implication and classical shibboleth, pervasive as it was, was strengthened, in effect, by a religious alliance.

The hexamerist commentators had long insisted that Adam's naming of the animals was a special function of his insight into their essential natures; not only does Milton enter this tradition when Adam tells Raphael that "I nam'd them, as they pass'd, and understood / Thir Nature" (VIII, 352-3), but it is apparently more real belief than hexamerist convention for the pamphleteer who, writing on divorce, could casually comment: "Adam . . . had the wisdom giv'n him to know all creatures, and to name them according to their properties."[28] Francis Bacon

---

[24] *An Humble Motion . . . Concerning the Advancement of Learning* (London, 1649), p. 34.

[25] *Proposition for the Advancement of Experimental Philosophy,* in *The English Writings of Abraham Cowley,* ed. A. R. Waller (Cambridge, 1906), II, 255.

[26] I have examined the tradition in relation to science more thoroughly in my introductory essay to Thomas Sprat, *History of the Royal Society,* ed. Jackson I. Cope and Harold Whitmore Jones (St. Louis, 1958), pp. xxv-xxxii.

[27] The matter is elaborated in A. C. Howell, "Res et Verba: Words and Things," *ELH,* XIII (1946), 131-42. George Williamson, *The Senecan Amble* (Chicago and London, 1951), pp. 109 n., 280, 287, corrects and adds to Howell's treatment.

[28] *Tetrachordon,* in *Complete Prose Works of John Milton,* ed. Don M. Wolfe, *et al.* (New Haven, 1953-   ), II, 602. Cf. *De doct. Christ.*: "Certainly without extraordinary wisdom he could not have given names to the whole animal creation with such a sudden intelligence. Gen. ii. 20" (CE, XV, 53). On the tradition in the commentators see George C. Taylor,

saw in paradisiacal knowledge the crucial symbol for the end sought by communication: "the true end of knowledge . . . is a restitution and reinvesting (in great part) of man to the sovereignty and power (for whensoever he shall be able to call the creatures by their true names he shall again command them) which he had in his first state of creation."[29] And it was Bishop John Wilkins, a good Baconian in many other respects as well, who finally repeated the performance of Adam and repaired the disintegration of Babel by preparing his *Essay Towards a Real Character, and a Philosophical Language,* where every word was significant in form of that for which it stands. Clearly in such a preoccupation, words are significative of "things" in an almost mystic sense. Most important, I think, are the religious bearings of the tradition. There were many strange results, one of the strangest being the Puritan tendency to make sober funerary anagrams upon the names of departed "Saints" which with unerring pertinence embraced the essential nature of the man; less consciously but scarcely less accurately than Adam, the Puritan parent clearly "saw" the word for the man.[30]

In George Fox the Quaker we find a blazing consciousness of having been projected into Adam's state which makes the New England anagrammatics pale games played by fallen children. In 1647 Fox attained to an apocalyptic experience: "I saw into that which was without end, and things which cannot be uttered, and of the greatness and infiniteness of the love of God, which cannot be expressed by words."[31] But a few months later Fox inevitably translated this experience into its obverse; from a

Milton's Use of Du Bartas (Cambridge, Mass., 1934), pp. 61-2, and Arnold Williams, *The Common Expositor: An Account of the Commentaries on Genesis, 1527-1633* (Chapel Hill, 1948), pp. 81-2.

[29] *Valerius Terminus,* in *The Philosophical Works of Francis Bacon,* ed. Spedding, Ellis, and Heath (London, 1876), III, 222.

[30] Harold Jantz, "The First Century of New England Verse," *Proc. of the American Antiquarian Society,* LIII (1943), 219-523.

[31] *The Journal of George Fox,* ed. John L. Nickalls (Cambridge, 1952), p. 21.

vision of the inexpressible nature of God he arrived at a capacity for the perfect expression. And it is notable that both occasions are described in linguistic terms: "being renewed up into the image of God by Jesus Christ, . . . I was come up to the state of Adam which he was in before he fell. The creation was opened to me, and it was showed me how all things had their names given them according to their nature and virtue."[32]

Not all Quakers perhaps might experience Fox's total mastery of the nature of things, but they all knew the inner value of names. The scriptural passage most germane to Quaker experience, and most frequently cited by witnesses, was the opening of the Johannine Gospel: "In the beginning was the Word, and the Word was with God, and the Word was God. . . . All things were made by him. . . . In him was life; and the life was the light of men. . . . *That* was the true light, which lighteth every man that cometh into the world. . . . to them gave he power to become the sons of God, *even* to them that believe on his name" (John 1:1-12).

It is clear enough that the Quakers did not develop any elaborate dogmatic theology based upon that religion of Protestants, the Bible; an important reason was their insistence upon the power of this Johannine Name, which was in the beginning the Word. Other Protestants seek the voice of God in the ancient Scriptures through "the Tongues, which makes their Divines, the beginning of which was Babel," says Fox. But he warns the Quakers that this is the way to error. Rather they must "feed upon the Milk of the Word, that was before Tongues, and see the ceasing of Tongues, and the beginning of Tongues, *Babel*, . . . thou must go before *Babel* and *Babylon* was . . . up into the Word Christ, whose Name is called the Word of God."[33]

Luke Howard, the shoemaker-soldier, who was successively

---

[32] *Journal* (anno 1648), p. 27.
[33] *A General Epistle To Be Read in All the Christian Meetings in the World* (n.p., 1662), pp. 11-2.

Brownist, Presbyterian, Independent, Baptist, and the first
Quaker in Kent, summed up the first chapter of John in a
great circle: "for the Word of God is the life of God, and the
life of God is the light of men, and the light of men is Jesus,
the Saviour of all which believe in him, and his Name is called
the Word of God, the entrance whereof giveth life."[34] William
Smith, the Nottingham pastor, oriented Scripture around the
"name" with even greater economy: "And here *Moses* and *John*
meet in unity, and their Testimony agrees in one, and all the
Dispensations and Administrations did hold forth this excellent
Glory which unto *John* was revealed in the Spirit; and from the
beginning to the end of all that is declared and written in so
many Words it is but a Testimony of him *whose Name is called
the Word of God,* Rev. 19 (Mark), the WORD is his Name,
and it was in the beginning, . . . all the Holy Men of God received it, . . . and they testified that there was not another
Name given whereby any could be saved."[35] Let us examine a
typical use of the "Name" in an exhortation to Friends by Fox
himself:

And so you that are gathered in the Name of Jesus, who have
bowed to the Name of Jesus, whose Name is called the Power of
God, and the Word, Light, Life and Truth; and for bowing to
his Name, for his Name sake have you suffered all along by
many powers; but the Name is a strong Tower: so who is bowed
to the Name, and gathered in the Name of the Lord, ye are in
the strong Tower, in which is safety and peace; for being gathered
in the Name of Christ Jesus, whose Name is above every Name,
for all things that was made, was made by Christ, whose Name
is above every Name, into his Name are you gathered; so above
all other names and gatherings are you gathered, who are gath-

[34] *A Few Plain Words of Instruction Given Forth as Moved of the Lord*
(London, 1658), p. 18.
[35] *The Morning-Watch: Or, A Spiritual Glass Opened* (London, 1660), pp.
11-2.

ered in the Name of Jesus Christ, by whom all things were made
and created; and being gathered in the Name of Jesus Christ by
which salvation is brought, by the Name of Christ, and not by
any other Name under Heaven, but by the Name of Jesus Christ
is salvation brought, by whom all things were made; for you being
gathered in this Name by which salvation is given, here you come
to be heirs of salvation, and then to inherit salvation, which is
Christ; *and by this you come to fathom all other names under the
whole Heaven,* and to see them, that there is no salvation in them;
and so likewise all other gatherings in all other names, no salvation in them; therefore cry people, There is no assurance of salvation upon earth, who are gathered in other names, but not in
the Name of Christ, by whom all things were made; and this is
the standing gathering in the Name, in the strong Tower, where
is the safety, where is the salvation, given and brought. Rejoice
ye all that are brought into this gathering, and have bowed to
the Name of Jesus.[36]

The stylistic features of such a repetition are an interesting
analogue to the concept of the "Name" itself as a central concept of Quaker theology. We find no varying of viewpoint, no
moving about the word to exhaust all of its facets of meaning
(as in the repetitions of Scripture words in the sermons of
Lancelot Andrewes and his epigoni); rather, the idea is logically
static throughout all of its repetitions. As Fox breasts forward
on the sound waves of his exhortation, he loses sight of the
grammatical structure. "And so you that are gathered in the
Name," he begins, but caught in the effect of his own repetition
of the old scriptural *logoi,* he is drawn away from his intention
into the vortex of this divine mystery, until through the word
itself he seems to see the light at its center. The "you" addressed does not receive the predication of action implied in
the opening. Instead, Fox discovers through this audience's
epithet, "gathered in the Name," not only the divinity which

[36] *A General Epistle,* pp. 1-2.

was in the beginning, but even that audience's participation in a time-conquering *stasis* of Christian perfection. What had begun as warning, instruction or exhortation to act becomes, through the hypnotic utterance of the divine names, a vision of human beatification for the Children of the Light. The incantation of the "Name" has undercut the progression implicit in grammar because it has revealed the heart of a world above time. This world and the other have been embodied in the Word.[37]

Paradoxically, it was just such enthusiasm as that of Fox which promoted John Wilkins' attempt at creating a universal language formally reflective of the real nature of things. Prefacing the *Essay* he explained that

> . . . this design will likewise contribute much to the clearing of some of our Modern differences in *Religion,* by unmasking many wild errors, that shelter themselves under the disguise of affected phrases; which being Philosophically unfolded, and rendered according to the genuine and natural importance of Words, will appear to be inconsistencies and contradictions.[38]

Wilkins did not succeed, of course, in clarifying anything at all through his immense labor of supererogation, but his effort points grimly to the dilemma which most effected the disturbances of interregnum and restoration England. No Quaker adapted Wilkins' linguistic translation of the nature of things because he already knew through his substantial scriptural "names." He had an Inner Light and stood under the high noon sun of the Day of the Lord. Like Wilkins, he was "come

---

[37] I discuss the nature and development of Quaker thought in this respect more elaborately in my essay "Seventeenth-Century Quaker Style," *PMLA,* LXXI (1956), 725-54.

[38] *An Essay Towards a Real Character, and a Philosophical Language* (London, 1668), sig. B, f. 1 (p. [ix]).

up to the state of Adam" before Babel to be confirmed in his faith by the new energy sensed in the creative power of the corporeal *word.*

Reaching desperately out of its hopeless religious polemics toward a universal truth, the seventeenth century tried to substitute metaphor for discursion. The Quakers are a touching example of this, hypnotizing themselves into a sensed grasp of truth by the very means which made them unintelligible to the world. But they were not alone. If they had an Inner Light in which all truth shown clearly forth, Nathaniel Culverwel, the Calvinist, saw as clearly that "There's scatter'd in the Soul of Man some seeds of light, which fill it with a vigorous pregnancy, with a multiplying fruitfulnesse, so that it brings forth a numerous and sparkling posterity of secondary notions." These seeds shower from the "heavenly beam which God has darted into the soul of man; from *the Candle of the Lord,* which God has lighted up for the discovery of his own Lawes."[39] With such a bright source, Culverwel might well wonder that any man could question the principles so clear in his exposition. But so might Benjamin Whichcote when he descries such a plain truth as that "Nothing *without* Reason is to be *proposed;* nothing *against* Reason is to be *believed:* Scripture is to be taken in a rational sense." The reasonable principles will again be clear to any man of good will, because "The *Spirit of a Man is the Candle of the Lord;* Lighted *by* God, and Lighting us *to* God. *Res illuminata, illuminans.*"[40] Henry More asserted that "it is sufficient to make a thing true according to the *light* of *Nature,* that no man upon a perception of what is propounded & the Reasons of it (if it be not clear at first sight, and need reasons to back it) will ever stick to acknowledge for a Truth."[41] But

[39] Nathaniel Culverwel, *An Elegant and Learned Discourse of the Light of Nature* (London, 1654), pp. 47, 59.

[40] "Aphorisms," in E. T. Campagnac, *The Cambridge Platonists* (Oxford, 1901), p. 70.

[41] *An Antidote against Atheism* (London, 1653), p. 32.

in the great circle of explanation, "reason" ever returns ultimately as that which makes things "clear." Indeed, no better index to the problem could be provided than More's language in this little passage. "Perception" authorizes the dangerous quasi-physical sense of the mental world implied in what Ong calls "the Ramist corpuscular epistemology," a sense more firmly implied by More's notion that the idea-as-object may perhaps be immediately "clear at first sight" through the illumination of "the *light* of *Nature.*" Writing on the most abstract of mental processes, More is ultimately dependent upon a metaphorical vocabulary which implies all of the poetic license of John Smith's Neoplatonic rhapsody: "Divinity indeed is a true Efflux from the Eternal light, which, like the Sun-beams, does not only enlighten, but heat and enliven; and therefore our Saviour hath in his *Beatitudes* connext Purity of heart with the Beatifical Vision. And as the Eye cannot behold the Sun, . . . unless it be *Sunlike*, and hath the form and resemblance of the Sun drawn in it; so neither can the Soul of man behold God, . . . unless it be *Godlike*, hath God formed in it."[42]

If we turn from theology to philosophy, from mid-century to its close, we can see in Locke's *Essay Concerning Human Understanding* a similar phenomenon. In the "Epistle to the Reader," Locke makes an effort to escape the metaphoric impasse to which his predecessors had been tending. "*Clear* and *distinct ideas*," he warns, "are terms which I have reason to think every one who uses does not perfectly understand. . . . I have therefore in most places chose to put *determinate* or *determined*, instead of *clear* and *distinct*, as more likely to direct men's thoughts to my meaning in this matter." But even as he proceeds to define his conception he begins to circle back upon the visual metaphor: "By those denominations, I mean some object in the mind, and consequently determined, i.e.,

---

[42] *A Discourse Concerning the True Way or Method of Attaining to Divine Knowledge*, in *Cambridge Platonists*, p. 80.

such as it is there seen and perceived to be."[43] And when he comes to his extended discussion "Of Clear and Obscure, Distinct and Confused Ideas" (II, xxix), Locke's opening definition is by way of a visual analogy which slips over unconsciously into metaphor once more when he smugly concludes, "This, I suppose, needs no application to make it plainer":

> The perception of the mind being most aptly explained by words relating to the sight, we shall best understand what is meant by *clear* and *obscure* in our ideas, by reflecting on what we call clear and obscure in the objects of sight. Light being that which discovers to us visible objects, we give the name of *obscure* to that which is not placed in a light sufficient to discover minutely to us the figure and colours which are observable in it, and which, in a better light, would be discernible.[44]

Later, of course, growing conscious of the limitations of this simplistic psychology, Locke would introduce the "association of ideas," and hence open the way to a modern sense of the fluid unconscious.[45] But the early version was extremely important in perpetuating for later generations the dilemma of metaphoric epistemology which was Locke's own inheritance from Ramism and the revolution of which it was the culmination:

> . . . unless we fully understand this matter of simple seeing by a clear light as reasoning, we cannot fully understand in what sense the age that followed Locke, whose philosopher he was, is the "Enlightenment"; . . . "To lay the naked ideas on which the force of the argumentation depends in their due order"—in

---

[43] John Locke, *An Essay Concerning Human Understanding*, ed. A. C. Fraser (Oxford, 1894), I, 22.

[44] Ibid., I, 486-7.

[45] Ernest Lee Tuveson, "Locke and the 'Dissolution of the Ego,'" *MP*, LII (1955), 159-74, brilliantly analyzes the stages of Locke's *Essay* for their impact upon later intellectual history, and it is to his analysis that I am largely indebted.

simplest terms, the arrangement of the pictures—this is the essential; once it is done, men can hardly fail to conclude aright.[46]

Certainly here we have one of the most significant results of Ramus' "habit of regarding everything, mental and physical, as composed of little corpuscular units . . . supposing that knowledge consists of sets of mental items."[47]

What has been developing is clearly a terrible paradox. It begins with the assumption that words should correspond to things. Ramus' motivation was, of course, like Locke's, clarity. "Now every idea a man has, being visibly what it is," wrote Locke, "and distinct from all other ideas but itself; that which makes it confused, is, when it is such that it may as well be called by another name as that which it is expressed by."[48]

Were such error to be overcome, the interior world would be-

---

[46] Ibid., p. 165.

[47] This corpuscular imagination is certainly the chief factor in that development of Renaissance thought which we are tracing. However, it must be observed that Ramus' influence cross-fertilized that of Christian metaphor even more particularly, that is, in the very matter of insisting upon "clarity" and encouraging the light imagery which that term implies. The 1572 edition of the *Dialecticae*, much changed from the earlier versions, had a "new accent on 'clarity.' . . . The quest for clarity . . . reveals its rhetorical, rather than logical, inspiration" (Ong, *Ramus*, p. 251). In brief, what is happening is that Ramus, writing primarily as a teacher, and in defense of his treatment of grammar, finds it safer to shift from the scientists' interest in what is in itself better known (*per se notius*) to what is more clear (*per se clarius*). It is difficult to assert that the definition of grammar is better known than the partition of grammar, but a practical teacher may well claim that the latter is "clearer" for pupils in the pedagogical process. Ong indicates that gradually the new term becomes a common factor in Ramistic thinking, and that it also gradually accumulates pretensions which our whole discussion has revealed as factors in the seventeenth-century crisis: "From here one could easily leap to the conclusion that the presentation proceeded from what was 'clearer' *of itself* [rather than pedagogically] or 'in the nature of things' and thereby 'more known.' To prove this conclusion was a difficult business and best not attempted. One simply supposed that 'clarity' (more or less as measured in the classroom) and intelligibility were one" (Ibid., p. 251). One lesser area into which this use of light imagery permeated to confuse discursive analysis was the vocabulary of the Renaissance aesthetic critic: see Tuve, *Elizabethan and Metaphysical Imagery*, pp. 29-32, 67.

[48] *Essay*, I, 488.

come visual, a great diagram mapping an objective reality, and words would be signs of size and relation upon that map, as they become upon the pages of Wilkins' *Essay Towards a Real Character, and a Philosophical Language.* But when we turn to Scripture, to matters spiritual, and find a Robert Ferguson saying that even there "under the most stately dress of words, there always lyes a richer quarry of things,"[49] the language may be that of Sprat's "so many *things,* almost in an equal number of *words,*" but the significance is crucially altered. Scripture deals with spiritual matters; Adam did not name the animals from their appearances, but "according to their properties," and "understood / Thir Nature." As one moves from Fox's projection of himself into this state echoed in the related cries from Quakerdom, one can perceive the poetic function of language reasserting itself over the significative, the word itself becoming the "thing." The paradox lies precisely in the origin of this iconoclastic and anticommunicative use of language in a strenuous and dedicated effort to repair the havoc worked by empty terms, sounding rhetoric. The terror lies in the fact that there was a long moment in which this poetic language existed without the re-creative rationale of a poem.

The intuitive experience was projected by the Cambridge Platonists, by the Quakers and enthusiasts like Everard or Muggleton, by John Locke, as "clear" ideas, "plain" truths, "the Light of Reason," "the Light of Nature," "the Inner Light," "the Candle of the Lord, *res illuminata, illuminans.*" These terms, of course, could not be explained discursively if they did not signify beyond themselves. But, as they were spiritual and epistemological metaphors, the only reference they carried was circular, back to that state of inner experience of which they were both creature and creator, a point nowhere more obvious than with the Quakers. So the futile, heartbreakingly sincere

---

[49] *The Interest of Reason in Religion* (London, 1675), p. 160.

polemic went on throughout the seventeenth century, each earn-
est champion making his own religious experience in an image
invisible to the others, in the most ironic sense "corporealizing"
words, and projecting them into a verbal icon for one's own
mind's eye alone.[50]

Milton did not escape this paradox; we find it plaguing him
throughout the *De doctrina Christiana.* His awareness of a
problem is indicated obliquely in his insistent apology for scriptural accommodation:

> When we speak of knowing God, it must be understood with
> reference to the imperfect comprehension of man; for to know
> God as he really is, far transcends the powers of man's thoughts,
> much more of his perception. I. Tim. vi. 16. "dwelling in the light
> which no man can approach unto.". . . granting that both in the
> literal and figurative descriptions of God, he is exhibited not as
> he really is, but in such a manner as may be within the scope
> of our comprehensions, yet we ought to entertain such a con-
> ception of him, as he, in condescending to accommodate himself
> to our capacities, has shown that we should conceive.[51]

It was a stance traditional but acutely difficult in Christian
exegetics; the discomfort is poignantly reflected in Calvin's turn-
ings about the communion: "It is a spiritual mystery, which
cannot be seen by the eye, nor comprehended by the human
understanding. It is therefore symbolized by visible signs, as

---

[50] Cf. the account of Anne Hutchinson's trial in Feidelson, *Symbolism and
American Literature,* pp. 94-5: "Since word, thought, and thing were one,
the controversialist could appeal only to immediate apprehension by the
'natural light' of reason and try to convince by demonstrating a necessary
meaning. To gain acceptance became increasingly difficult." Cf. also the account of Edwards' attempts to escape the dilemma through symbolizing nature,
pp. 99-101. Basil Willey, *The Seventeenth Century Background* (London,
1934; New York, 1942), pp. 133-69, 245, 254, *et passim,* on the other hand,
seems to consider the seventeenth century to be freeing itself from, rather than
intensifying, the dilemma "between pictorial and conceptual thinking."

[51] *CE,* XIV, 31-3.

our infirmity requires, but in such a way that it is not a bare figure, but joined to its reality and substance."[52]

Milton's treatise frequently reflects the difficulty. For instance, when he speaks of "Man's Renovation, including his Calling," he finds "the natural mind and will of man being partially renewed by a divine impulse. . . . Inasmuch as this change is from God, those in whom it takes place are said to be enlightened. . . . As this change is of the nature of an effect produced on man, and an answer, as it were, to the call of God, it is sometimes spoken of under the metaphor of hearing or hearkening."[53] But in his discussion of the Holy Spirit, we discover that these same metaphors act as definition. In Scripture, Milton recalls, the *spiritus sanctus* sometimes "means that impulse or voice of God by which the prophets were inspired"; "Sometimes it means that light of truth, . . . wherewith God enlightens and leads his people"; or it may be defined as "a divine impulse, or light, or voice, or word, transmitted from above."[54] In brief, Milton is not delineating the process of vocation by mere illustrative metaphor, as his statement would suggest, but according to the difficult Calvinist mystique, treating it as "not a bare figure, but joined to its reality and substance." And one can scarcely determine whether it is rhetoric or argument for Milton when he writes:

> The very essence of Truth is plainnesse, and brightnes; the darknes and crookednesse is our own. The *wisdome* of *God* created *understanding*, fit and proportionable to Truth the object, and end of it, as the eye to the thing visible. If our *understanding*

---

[52] *Calvin: Theological Treatises*, ed. J. K. S. Reid (Philadelphia, 1954), p. 147. I am indebted to the treatment in Roland Mushat Frye, *God, Man, and Satan: Patterns of Christian Thought and Life in Paradise Lost, Pilgrim's Progress, and the Great Theologians* (Princeton, 1960), pp. 8-17. Cf. also the good discussion in Edward A. Dowey, *The Knowledge of God in Calvin's Theology* (New York, 1952), pp. 3-4, *et passim*.

[53] *CE*, XV, 353-5.

[54] *CE*, XIV, 361-7.

have a film of *ignorance* over it, or be blear with gazing on other false glisterings, what is that to Truth? If we will but purge with sovrain eyesalve that intellectual ray which *God* hath planted in us, then we would beleeve the Scriptures protesting their own plainnes, and perspicuity . . .[55]

The images of his argument are themselves drawn from the argument of the source.

But if metaphor is the clay of poetry, poetry is the inspiration of metaphor. The immediate and intuitive language, which frustrates the religious polemicist in discursive argument is precisely the "corporeal" word out of which the poet reshapes reality. Metaphors of light and darkness, blindness and vision, falling and rising are only the invisible counters of private insight in theology, even for a Milton. Yet, released from meaning into being, from the paths of argument into the patterns of poetry, these *topoi* became in Milton's voice that great metaphor which we have found the critics of our own age seeking as the ideal culmination of the poet's challenge to the limits of language. I have attempted to disentangle some of the forces which urged Milton's talents toward the making of that ideal poem. In the remainder of this book I will essay to view those structures which justify the epithet "metaphoric" for *Paradise Lost* with peculiar force.

[55] *Of Reformation,* in *Prose Works,* I, 566.

III

TIME AND SPACE
AS MILTONIC SYMBOL

I

PROFESSOR MARJORIE NICOLSON is fond of quoting Masson's observation that "Shakespeare lived in a world of time, Milton in a universe of space."[1] This notion provided her with a focus for the influential and exciting essay in which she suggested that "Milton's imagination . . . was stimulated less by *books about* the new astronomy than by the *actual sense experience* of celestial observation. . . . Milton on some occasion 'viewed all things at one view' through a telescope. . . . That experience he never forgot . . . it made *Paradise Lost* the first modern cosmic poem in which a drama is played against a background of interstellar space."[2] In a later study, tracing the

---

[1] "Milton and the Telescope," *ELH*, II (1935); reprinted in *Science and Imagination* (Ithaca, 1956), p. 96.

[2] Ibid., p. 81; Elmer Edgar Stoll has argued against Nicolson's viewpoint in "Criticism Criticized: Spenser and Milton," *JEGP*, XLI (1942), pp. 451-77, and in *From Shakespeare to Joyce* (New York, 1944), pp. 413-21. His criticism fails to convince me, however, when it reduces Milton's spatial descriptions to a commonplace of literary tradition. Kester Svendsen, "Satan and Science," *Bucknell Review*, IX (1960), 130-42, emphasizes the aesthetic potency of Milton's space by reference to the interesting plates of John Martin,

breaking of the circle of perfection which had enclosed the
medieval world, Professor Nicolson went on to elaborate the
paradox that Milton was aesthetically gratified by that infinity
which he rejected on theological grounds.[3] Certainly no reader
of *Paradise Lost* has failed to sense that ever-present shifting of
a spatial perspective moving through vast immensities which
lends substance to such observations. And most readers will
have followed Professor Nicolson's argument into *Paradise Regained,* where she finds a succession of views which are "limited
to this world alone, even though the scope of some of them is
such as to stagger comprehension."[4] The chief of these, of
course, is the scene of temptation on the mountain, a scene to
which we will return.

These seem to me valuable and pertinent analyses, which
describe the spatial aspect of Milton's poetry as a cultural
phenomenon reflecting that vision of nature which was opening
out around the poet. We must recollect, however, that while
space forces itself upon the astronomer or painter, it is not equally
necessary for the poet to come to terms with this dimension.
Milton's very early employment of movement toward the widen-
ing heavens, as apotheosis-symbol in the "Fair Infant" and as
the ladder to prophecy in "Il Penseroso," warns us that we
should not tacitly attribute to Galileo's space the same significance that is attached to that which expands from the pages of
an epic. I should like to examine the spatial dimension of *Paradise Lost,* therefore, not as a cultural osmosis by which contemporary reality seeps into literature, but as the aesthetic shape
of the myth through which Milton created *meaning* for the
boundless spaces viewed by Galileo "At Ev'ning from the top of

---

the early nineteenth-century illustrator of *Paradise Lost*. Cf. also Walter Clyde
Curry, *Milton's Ontology, Cosmogony, and Physics* (Lexington, 1957), pp.
144-57.
    [3] *The Breaking of the Circle* (Evanston, 1950), pp. 160-6.
    [4] *Science and Imagination,* pp. 93-4.

Fesole." And to do so, I must turn from the stirring new commonplaces of seventeenth-century science to an older tradition of literary *topoi.*

Patch documented the ubiquity of the goddess Fortuna's association with the sea in the literature of the Middle Ages,[5] and Renaissance readers, familiar with the sonneteers' complaints for their love-tossed ship of fate or with the reiteration of the Lucretian safe haven in *The Faerie Queene,* needed no G. Wilson Knight to explicate for them the Shakespearean tempests. Even more familiar is the image of Fortune's wheel, on which was spun the massive "Fall of Princes" literature which blankets both Middle Ages and Renaissance. These are threadbare metaphors. But Professor Stephen Gilman has given us an exciting and perceptive study of Fernando de Rojas' *La Celestina* which demonstrates that Rojas utilized the old *topoi* not as metaphors for fortune, but as the spatialization of fortune into plot.[6] In this magnificent *tragicomedia* of the closing years of the fifteenth century, the lover Calisto makes a misstep from a ladder to Melibea's window and tumbles to his death — ironically, in that he was scurrying toward the clamor of some ruffians who, contracted to kill him, had decided instead merely to set up the confused sounds of a fight in order to frighten Calisto, discretion being the better part of their cowardly valor.

The death of the heroine Melibea intensifies the ironic transmutation of the tropes of *Fortuna.* Anguished at Calisto's death,

---

[5] Howard Patch, *The Goddess Fortuna in Medieval Literature* (Cambridge, Mass., 1927), pp. 101-7.

[6] *The Art of La Celestina* (Madison, 1956), pp. 119-93. The interested reader should also consult Leo Spitzer, "A New Book on the Art of 'The Celestina,'" *Hispanic Review,* XXV (1957), 1-25, a violent attack upon several points in Gilman's study, including the interpretation of the falls. Gilman successfully replied in "A Rejoinder to Leo Spitzer," *Hispanic Review,* XXV (1957), 112-21, and expanded his argument in "The Fall of Fortune from Allegory to Fiction," *Filologia Romanza,* IV (1957), 337-54.

Melibea tricks her father into allowing her to ascend to the house top to view the ships in the distance: "Subamos, Señor, al açotea alta, por que desde allí goze de la deleytosa vista de los nauíos." Here are the ships of fortune on a physical horizon, an extraordinary touch which has given rise to a large corpus of debate among the literal-minded who seek to identify the unspecified "place" of *La Celestina* through the key offered by "la ribera" on which these ships float. But Melibea leaps toward them to her death, and her father's lamentations make it clear that the ships, like the fall, are symbols: "¿Para quien edifiqué torres? . . . ¿Para quien fabriqué navíos? ¡O fortuna variable, ministra é mayordoma de los temporales bienes! ¿Por qué no executaste tu cruel yra, tus mudables ondas, en aquello que á tí es subjeto?"

Leaving Professor Gilman's skillful argument undeveloped, we must return to *Paradise Lost,* and admit that the falling through "el ayre ageno y extraño" toward the river of *La Celestina* leaves nothing like the impression of space which surrounds the reader of Milton's epic. If I understand her argument correctly, Professor Nicolson would account for Milton's greater preoccupation with space as his heritage from a scientific age whose expanding universe led Newton to argue for a God "all eye, all ear," who "in infinite space, as it were in his sensory, sees the things themselves intimately, and thoroughly perceives them."[7] But realizing that Milton, unlike his Cambridge contemporary Henry More, does not choose to equate

---

[7] I cite Newton's *Optics* from Edwin A. Burtt, *The Metaphysical Foundations of Modern Physical Science* (London, 1950), p. 284. Cf. John Tull Baker, *An Historical and Critical Examination of English Space and Time Theories from Henry More to Bishop Berkeley* (Bronxville, 1930); Nicolson, *The Breaking of the Circle;* Rosalie L. Colie, "Thomas Traherne and the Infinite: The Ethical Compromise," *HLQ,* XXI (1957), 69-82; and another study by Professor Colie which bears similar implications for Milton: "Time and Eternity: Paradox and Structure in *Paradise Lost,*" *JWCI,* XXII (1960), 127-38.

God's infinity with an infinite space,[8] let us look inward, as Gilman has done with *La Celestina,* toward space as symbol in the poem rather than outward toward the cosmology of those scientists and enthusiasts whom Professor Nicolson has so aptly called the "romantics" of Milton's age.

II

> . . . what surmounts the reach
> Of human sense, I shall delineate so,
> By lik'ning spiritual to corporal forms,
> As may express them best (V, 571-4),

explains Milton's Raphael. He speaks of war in heaven, but he has no difficulty in delineating action; the trouble lies in the depiction of heaven as place. Lying outside of space, it cannot be captured in any metaphors of substance. The jasper before the throne is now a "bright / Pavement" (III, 362-3); now it "flows" around Jacob's Ladder (III, 518-9); in another moment it is even indeterminate whether "a bright Sea flow'd / Of Jasper, or of liquid Pearle" (III, 518-9). Like details are only echoes of the uncertainty of the whole prospect of heaven as it lies "extended wide / In circuit, undetermin'd square or round" (II, 1047-8). Such descriptions are not even approximations in the sense that metaphor approximates, because they result in the paradox of contradiction.

---

[8] "Milton's theology, on the whole, . . . draws from a tradition which is antithetic to that which was at least temporarily to triumph in establishing in the seventeenth century a theory of infinite universe as the inevitable expression of infinite Deity, the essence of whose Nature is the overflowing goodness that must show itself in the creation of all possible forms of existence in the created universe. Had he expressed himself on the subject in the *Treatise of Christian Doctrine,* there is little doubt that he would have denied the possibility of infinite space" (Nicolson, *Science and Imagination,* p. 107).

We are likely to remember the magnificent description of Christ creating in chaos on that occasion when:

He took the golden Compasses, . . .
. . . to circumscribe
This Universe, . . .

. . . . .
And said, thus far extend, thus far thy bounds,
This be thy just Circumference, O World (VII, 225-31).

But we are not so likely to recall that as Christ and his angels set out to accomplish this creative act,

They view'd the vast immeasurable Abyss
Outrageous as a Sea, dark, wasteful, wild,
Up from the bottom turn'd by furious winds
And surging waves, . . . (VII, 211-4).

The same image confronted Satan and Sin when she threw back hell's gate and

Before thir eyes in sudden view appear
The secrets of the hoary deep, a dark
Illimitable Ocean without bound,
Without dimension, where length, breadth, and highth,
And time and place are lost (II, 890-4).

The old metaphor of the raging sea should alert us: time and place are lost in heaven and chaos alike, but the one transcends space and time, the other reluctantly gives them birth. Thus the dimensionless quality of chaos parodies that of heaven, even as the golden turrets of Pandemonium parody those of the celestial city. And if Christ creates a world from chaos, it is a second creation, God's concession to the evil of that great fall of Satan at the end of which "Nine times the Space that measures Day and Night / To mortal men, he with his horrid crew / Lay vanquisht" (I, 50-2). The Father is explicit on this point, explaining that he is reacting to "repair / That detriment" left in heaven by Satan "lest his heart exalt him in the harm / Already done" (VII, 150-6). Having validated icons by looking with self-idolatry into the mirror provided by Sin, Satan has validated also the medium in which icons must exist, the medium in which his spiritual distance from the "most High" must be perceived in the image of the fall: space. The "reaction" of God is both real and merely apparent according to whether we view it from time or in eternity. The final cause of material creation, of course, cannot be Satan; the great spaces of the worlds shall be turned to serve God's glory first and last, even as will Satan himself. But in the interim, the obverse of the paradox must be allowed to assert itself in order that the structure of divine irony can be finally realized.

I suggest that chaos is the great sea of fortune in which Satan thrashes his Icarian wings to cast up the world's first pair of star-crossed lovers and that vast space across which they pursue the passage of their death-marked love.[9] For every-

---

[9] My interpretation, derived from the internal structures of the epic, reinforces the analyses of other historians who have found discrepancies between *Paradise Lost* and *De doctrina Christiana*, reminding us again that we cannot read a theologian's poem as theology. On this point I prefer the statement by B. Rajan, *Paradise Lost and the Seventeenth Century Reader*, pp. 25-38. The particular difficulty is Milton's stand against *ex nihilo* creation in the treatise, where he concludes that "the original matter of which we speak is not to be looked upon as an evil or trivial thing, but as intrinsically good" (CE, XV, 53). Even here, however, the phrasing, when contrasted with the enthusiasm of More or Newton or Traherne, suggests reluctance. Some careful examinations have been made. Arthur Sewell argued that the divergency between poem and compendium concerning matter was owing to a chronological shift in Milton's over-all views, confusedly reflected in a *De doctrina* which was never thoroughly integrated, being made up of parts from two different eras in Milton's thinking (*A Study in Milton's Christian Doctrine* [Oxford, 1939], pp. 10-4, 40, 127-32, 170-3). Maurice Kelley's *This Great Argument* (Princeton, 1941) cast much doubt upon Sewell's chronological thesis, but did not come to grips with his discussion of Milton's conception of matter. A. S. P.

where in the epic cosmos, space is the vehicle of imperfection and of pain. The most terrible awareness of this state comes through the fierce irony of the fallen angels' attempts to regain heaven by re-creating its every detail in the matter of hell. As the almost numberless parallels between the two regions are developed, we come to realize that the metaphor of extension in which Milton and Raphael speak of heaven has become diabolical reality.[10] But except in the language of paradox, heaven defies expression for Satan even as for Raphael:

> While they adore me on the Throne of Hell,
> With Diadem and Sceptre high advanc'd
> The lower still I fall . . . (IV, 89-91).

We notice that the first instance of the intricate interplay of ironic parallels between heaven and hell appears with the first movement made by a creature through created space. Satan fallen arises to go toward the flaming shore of hell with "uneasy steps / Over the burning Marl, not like those steps / On Heaven's Azure" (I, 295-7). Henceforth, painful effort is omni-

---

Woodhouse, "Notes on Milton's Views of Creation: The Initial Phases," *PQ*, XXVIII (1949), 211-36, argues that even in *De doctrina* "the mark of the potentiality of the first matter is its disorder" (p. 224), while in *Paradise Lost* "it is difficult to escape the inference, denied in the treatise, that this disorder is, or at all events has some affinity with, evil" (p. 229). Woodhouse suggests the possibility of influence from Methodius and Robert Fludd. Peter F. Fisher, "Milton's Theodicy," *JHI*, XVII (1956), 28-53, esp. 37-9, 41-3, 47-53 traces a struggle to unify persistently diverging metaphysical and theological tendencies concerning the relation of matter to evil, to darkness, and to chaos. Walter Clyde Curry, *Milton's Ontology*, pp. 48-73, esp. 60 ff., argues circumstantially, but less convincingly than Fisher, that Milton's presentation of matter in relation to chaos and night derives from the Neoplatonic theologies. Cf. also William B. Hunter, Jr., "Milton's Power of Matter," *JHI*, XIII (1952), 551-62, on Christian interpreters' problems in adapting the Aristotelian conception of form-matter relations. Broadbent, *Some Graver Subject*, pp. 209-10, 215-6, sees contradiction as aesthetic failure, and misses the symbolic context.

[10] Cf. Arnold Stein, *Answerable Style*, pp. 17-37, esp. 31, 35-7, 43. Stein also is trenchant on Adam's materialistic orientation, pp. 78, 82.

present in the creation: Satan's journey through the primal matter is an epitome of the point:

> . . . nigh founder'd on he fares,
> Treading the crude consistence, half on foot,
> Half flying . . .
>
> .   .   .   .
>
> O'er bog or steep, through strait, rough, dense, or rare,
> With head, hands, wings, or feet pursues his way,
> And swims or sinks, or wades, or creeps, or flies (II, 940-50).

If space is the ambient of pain, called into being by Satan's fall, it is however not forgotten by the poet that it was the Father who "bid the Deep / Within appointed bounds be Heav'n and Earth" (VII, 166-7), and Christ who "circumscribe[d] / This Universe" (VII, 226-7). For there is a consistent connotative antithesis throughout the poem between circumscription and spaciousness.[11] At the Father's announcement of Christ's exaltation, the angels summoned from the corners of heaven with their "Ten thousand thousand Ensignes high advanc'd" press in about the throne, until "in Orbs / Of circuit inexpressible they stood, / Orb within Orb" (V, 594-6). Eden is an encased jewel crowning the head "Of a steep wilderness, whose hairy sides / With thicket overgrown, grotesque and wild, / Access deni'd" (IV, 135-7). Even in hell circumscription is symbolic of order. As Book One closes, and Pandemonium rises, we survey first its outer face: "where *Pilasters* round / Were set" (713-4). Then "straight the doors / Op'ning thir brazen folds discover wide / Within, her ample spaces" (723-5); the devils swarm inside, diminishing their size, so that:

---

[11] The symbolic values of "space" and of "spaciousness" have not been quite thoroughly distinguished at one point. Chaos is revealed as the reluctant womb of space (II, 915-6, 998-1006), because creation implies an ordering and circumscribing of realms formerly under confused dominion. And yet, this same "space" is itself the vehicle of disorder and confusion in its frequent role of "spaciousness." Cf. the comments by Woodhouse cited in note nine above.

incorporeal Spirits to smallest forms
Reduc'd thir shapes immense, and were at large,
Though without number still amidst the Hall
Of that infernal Court (789-92).

Just as the angels of hell are gradually losing their heavenly
luster, so they are gradually throwing aside the shock of their
brush with chaos. As space and matter are compressed through
the funnel-form movement of this perspective with which we
enter Pandemonium, hell ceases to be merely experience and becomes a monarchy:

. . . But far within
And in thir own dimensions like themselves
The great Seraphic Lords and Cherubim
In close recess and secret conclave sat (792-5).

Contrasting with the order indicated by circumscription,
spaciousness is the natural milieu of disorder and evil. In heaven
Satan gathers his armies and ambitions "throughout the spacious
North" (V, 726), and his troops challenge the forces of heaven
from this distant perspective:

. . . over many a tract
Of Heav'n they march'd, and many a Province wide
Tenfold the length of this terrene: at last
Far in th' Horizon to the North appear'd
From skirt to skirt a fiery Region, . . . (VI, 76-80).

In hell, fast upon the initial fall, Satan's first prospect and ours
stretches into indefinite distances: "At once as far as Angels
ken he views / The dismal Situation waste and wild" (I, 59-60).
This at the poem's opening. As it closes, after the second fall,
with Adam and Eve's expulsion "down the Cliff . . . / To the

subjected Plain," "The World was all before them" (XII, 639-46).

The most striking passage of spatial perspective in *Paradise Lost*, however, comes at neither beginning nor end. It comes at that climactic moment of the argument, in which God himself justifies his ways to man, even as he foretells the fall:

> Now had the Almighty Father from above,
> From the pure Empyrean where he sits
> High Thron'd above all highth, bent down his eye,
> His own works and their works at once to view:
>
> .   .   .   .
>
> . . . On Earth he first beheld
> Our two first Parents, yet the only two
> Of mankind, in the happy Garden plac't,
>
> .   .   .   .
>
> . . . he then survey'd
> Hell and the Gulf between, and *Satan* there
> Coasting the wall of Heav'n on this side Night
> In the dun Air sublime, and ready now
> To stoop with wearied wings, and willing feet
> On the bare outside of this World, that seem'd
> Firm land imbosom'd without Firmament,
> Uncertain which, in Ocean or in Air.
> Him God beholding from his prospect high,
> Wherein past, present, future he beholds,
> Thus to his only Son foreseeing spake (III, 56-79).

What strikes one is that God is looking at that history which he will proceed to explain in his articulation of the fortunate fall. Time has become space, because space is at once the creature, the ambient and the symbol of that fall in which Milton found the meaning of nature's history and of man's.

Yet it is a *fortunate* fall, owing to that divine benevolence

"That all this good of evil shall produce / And evil turn to good" (XII, 470-1). Space is a dimension which both Satan in his way and man in his are attempting to transcend. Satan, "Self-tempted, self-deprav'd" can only forever continue shaping and reshaping the metaphor of matter into a dead image of heaven. But for man, space, like the fall, is a paradox. Stigma of his imperfection, it is yet to be made the instrument of his glory. With him, space will itself one day become spirit. Men fall to rise,

> . . . till by degrees of merit rais'd
> They open to themselves at length the way
> Up hither, under long obedience tri'd,
> And Earth be chang'd to Heav'n, and Heav'n to Earth,
> One Kingdom, Joy and Union without end (VII, 157-61).[12]

Even as the first parents were hurried down the cliff to the plain they had begun the ascent, for,

> The World was all before them, where to choose
> Thir place of rest, and Providence thir guide (XII, 646-7).

III

IN AN OBVIOUS and important sense, we may find *Paradise Regained* spatially oriented as well as *Paradise Lost*. As the poem opens, Christ is "our Morning Star then in his rise" (I, 294). The symbol flows into the poem from the icons of history, but acts particularly, too, as Milton's own internal symbol and imagistic frame. The action rises *literally* toward two climaxes: the vision of the kingdoms of the world from the putative Mount Niphates, and the temptation on the pinnacle of the

12 Cf. III, 323-41.

temple in Jerusalem. There, amid the "golden spires," the spiraling of temptations culminates physically. It is a fit conclusion, which finds a desperate Satan taking the battle into his own element, that space which the devils have conquered to become "ancient Powers of Air and this wide world" (I, 44).[13] But as our Morning Star rises to "begin to save mankind" (IV, 635) he for the second time sends Satan hurtling from the towers of a glittering holy city: "Tempt not the Lord thy God; he said and stood. / But Satan smitten with amazement fell / . . . Fell whence he stood to see his Victor fall" (IV, 561-2, 571).[14] It is the type and promise of the larger pattern foreseen by the choir of angels who at the poem's close hymn mercy and promise justice: "thou, Infernal Serpent, shalt not long / Rule in the Clouds; like an Autumnal Star / . . . thou shalt fall from Heav'n trod down / Under his feet" (IV, 618-21).

And yet a reader who moves from *Paradise Lost* into *Paradise Regained* feels involved in a totally different aesthetic medium. There are the same journeys into heaven, into the "middle Region of thick Air," but they are journeys through a world without perspective. We hear of flight, we do not view it. Satan, we are told, "roving still / About the world . . . Flies to his place, nor rests, but in mid air / To Council summons all his mighty Peers" (I, 33-40). Leaving this meeting, "to the Coast of *Jordan* he directs / His easy steps" (I, 119-20). Once there, the archfiend appears suddenly on the desert (I, 314-9), and disappears as suddenly at the close of his first attempt upon Christ: "Satan, bowing low / His gray dissimulation, disappear'd / Into thin Air diffus'd" (I, 497-9). In *The Tempest*

---

[13] The diabolical tenancy of space is emphasized repeatedly: I, 44-50, 364-6; II, 116-20.

[14] Cf. Northrop Frye, "The Typology of *Paradise Regained*," MP, LIII (1956), 236, who comments on the last temptation: "Mentally, then, Christ is being tested for *hybris,* or pride of mind. He is in the position of a tragic hero, on top of the wheel of fortune, subject to the fatal instant of distraction that will bring him down."

Ariel comes as a harpy and "claps his wings" to dissipate a visionary banquet. The demonic banquet of *Paradise Regained* disappears with not the sight, but the sound only of the harpies:

> . . . With that
> Both Table and Provision vanish'd quite
> With sound of Harpies' wings, and Talons heard (II, 401-3).

Such a description leads us across the border from the unperspectived space, in which the poem's action subsists, to the lack of dimension given the very actors and objects which people it. "Though in his face / The glimpses of his Fathers glory shine" (I, 92-3), we never *see* Christ; God, the eye and arm of *Paradise Lost,* materializes himself only in a single adjective when he "smiling spake" (I, 129); Satan comes "now an aged man in Rural weeds" (I, 314), and returns "Not rustic as before, but seemlier clad, / As one in City, or Court, or Palace bred" (II, 299-300) — negligible descriptions after the mighty transformations of *Paradise Lost.* But the point is also made by juxtaposing related descriptions from the two poems. The banquet which Satan produces to tempt Christ is on:

> A Table richly spread, in regal mode,
> With dishes pil'd, and meats of noblest sort
> And savour, Beasts of chase, or Fowl of game,
> In pastry built, or from the spit, or boil'd,
> Gris-amber-steam'd; all Fish from Sea or Shore,
> Freshet, or purling Brook, of shell or fin (II, 340-5).

This is a nonpictorial, almost abstract passage which invites us to ignore the question of what Christ might have eaten and to pursue the idea that Satan parodied God's plenitude.[15]

---

[15] This interpretation, incidentally, answers Lamb's objections in "Grace Before Meat," *Works of Charles Lamb,* ed. A. Ainger (London, 1899), J,

Now contrast Eve's preparations to feed the angel Raphael in Paradise:

> . . . fruit of all kinds, in coat,
> Rough, or smooth rin'd, or bearded husk, or shell
> She gathers, Tribute large, and on the board
> Heaps with unsparing hand; for drink the Grape
> She crushes, inoffensive must, and meaths
> From many a berry, and from sweet kernels prest
> She tempers dulcet creams, . . . (V, 341-7).

Here the multiple assaults upon taste, touch, and smell smother the realization that Eve finds all the future plenitude of the wide earth in her isolated prelapsarian garden. And we find similar contrasts wherever we turn in the twin poems: Adam and Eve appear to Satan's view and ours in an elaborate description which metaphorically entwines them with the fertile flora of Eden (IV, 288-324); in *Paradise Regained* the beauties whom Belial and his "lusty Crew" "coupl'd with . . . and begot a race" (II, 153-204) are historic myths whose names, not charms, allure us, as are the "Nymphs of *Diana's* train . . . And Ladies of th' *Hesperides*" (II, 355-7) who dance beyond Christ's banquet table. As there is no depth to the spatial dimension which is the symbolic framework of the temptations, so there is no depth to the sensual matter of the temptations or to the physical guises of tempter and tempted: style as well as plot is calculated to focus upon the dialectic of logic and morality.

Professor Nicolson's discovery that *Paradise Regained* presents a succession of views of such scope "as to stagger comprehension" would seem to run counter to the dimensionless world which I have been reviewing. Examination of these perspective

---

191-2. I am aware that "plenitude" can only be loosely applied to Milton's conception of variety in creation: see A. O. Lovejoy, *The Great Chain of Being* (Cambridge, Mass., 1936), pp. 160-5.

descriptions, however, reveals a treatment at great variance with that which one finds in *Paradise Lost,* and serves, I think, to tell us more precisely how theme and style are interacting.

The first two books of *Paradise Regained* contain only the most negligible landscape perspectives: Christ walks into the "bordering Desert wild, / . . . with dark shades and rocks environ'd round," (I, 193-4), and immediately falls into meditation. We learn that he is "step by step led on," but what we actually read of is "Thought following thought" (I, 192). Later we hear a catalogue of cities named where Andrew and Simon sought the wandering Christ (II, 18-25), and for just a moment we stand with Christ on a hill to:

> ken the prospect round,
> If Cottage were in view, Sheep-cote or Herd;
> But Cottage, Herd or Sheep-cote none he saw,
> Only in a bottom saw a pleasant Grove (II, 286-9).

That is all in the way of "views" until we come to the climactic vision of the kingdoms which raises the poem to a higher level of intensity near the middle of Book Three.[16] Suddenly we are at a dizzy altitude, almost above the world whose "circuit wide" Christ scans (III, 251-64). Satan begins immediately to identify the scene in an exotic catalogue:

[16] Milton's own allusion to Christ's view of the kingdoms will remind the reader of *Paradise Lost* that Michael took Adam to "a Hill / Of Paradise the highest" (XI, 377-8) for another extensive vision. I omit that long section of the earlier epic from my discussion, however, because Adam is not viewing his surroundings even nominally. Rather, Michael's visual purge "pierc'd, / Ev'n to the inmost seat of *mental* sight" (XI, 417-8; italics mine), allowing Adam to view a cinematic chronicle rather than scene. The physical eye sees only the cities and empires catalogued before Adam enters his trance (XI, 385-411). The fact that none of these kingdoms exist at the moment of Adam's vision (a fact pertinent because the poem here is centered upon historical awareness of time), as well as the syntax, leads me to believe that the initial catalogue indicates not what Adam saw, but what Christ saw when "the Tempter set / Our second *Adam* in the Wilderness, / To show him all Earth's Kingdoms and thir Glory" (XI, 382-4).

> . . . here thou behold'st
> *Assyria* and her Empire's ancient bounds,
> *Araxes* and the *Caspian* lake, thence on
> As far as *Indus* East, *Euphrates* West (III, 269-72),

but almost imperceptibly the identifications become historical:

> Here *Ninevee*, of length within her wall
> Several days' journey, built by *Ninus* old,
> Of that first golden Monarchy the seat,
> And seat of *Salmanassar*, whose success
> *Israel* in long captivity still mourns (III, 275-9).

This historicism asserts itself fully as Satan points finally to the great Parthian empire. As the glistening cavalry pours from the gates of Ctesiphon, the tempter excitedly congratulates Christ on having been fortunate in the *timing* of his survey:

> All these the *Parthian*, now some Ages past,
> By great *Arsáces* led, who founded first
> That Empire, under his dominion holds
> From the luxurious Kings of *Antioch* won.
> And just in time thou com'st to have a view
> Of his great power; for now the *Parthian* King
> In *Ctesiphon* hath gather'd all his Host
> Against the *Scythian*, whose incursions wild
> Have wasted *Sogdiana*; to her aid
> He marches now in haste; see, though from far,
> His thousands, . . . (III, 294-304).

The spatial distances have been rapidly absorbed into the funnel of history, and it is history which Christ sees. Space has become time. In the Fourth Book, Milton twice repeats the technique. Moving to "the western side / Of that high mountain" (IV, 25-6), Christ surveys another plain, the glorious city of Rome, and "Embassies from Regions far remote / In various habits on the *Appian* road" (IV, 67-8); Satan catalogues the provinces whence they come, then in a moment he is describing Tiberius' career on *Capreae*, "with purpose there / His horrid lusts in private to enjoy" (IV, 93-4). The whole technique is repeated yet once more "ere we leave this specular Mount" when Christ looks at Athens only to have the scene quickly dissipate into a vision of history:

> See there the Olive Grove of *Academe*
> *Plato's* retirement, . . .
>
> .   .   .   .
> . . . there *Illissus* rolls
> His whispering stream; within the walls then view
> The schools of ancient Sages; his who bred
> Great *Alexander* to subdue the world,
> *Lyceum* there, and painted *Stoa* next;
> There thou shalt hear and learn the secret power
> Of harmony in tones and numbers . . .
>
> .   .   .   .
> And his who gave them breath, but higher sung,
> Blind *Melesigenes* thence *Homer* call'd,
> Whose Poem *Phoebus* challeng'd for his own.
> Thence what the lofty grave Tragoedians taught
> In *Chorus* or *Iambic*, teachers best . . . (IV, 244-63).

Enhancing the temporal usurpation of the normal spatial quality of these perspectives are Satan's interspersed and insistent explanations that it is all an optical illusion, a magic mirror of history, "strange Parallax or Optic skill / Of vision multiplied through air" (IV, 40-1); or the action of an "Aery Microscope" through which "thou may'st behold / Outside and inside both" (IV, 57-8). But more effective yet is the tempter's casual "let pass, as they are transitory, / The Kingdoms of this world" (IV, 209-10); or his stage-direction: "All these . . . in a moment thou behold'st" (IV, 162). It is only as the poem closes upon the final violent act of Satan that we begin to move in a world of unambiguous physical space reminiscent of *Paradise Lost*. There is the cosmic storm in the desert (IV, 409-25) which Christ calmly weathers; then the final flight in which Satan lifts Christ:

> . . . through the Air sublime
> Over the Wilderness and o'er the Plain;
> Till underneath them fair *Jerusalem,*
> The holy City, lifted high her Towers,
> And higher yet the glorious Temple rear'd
> Her pile, far off appearing like a Mount
> Of Alabaster, top't with golden Spires:
> There on the highest Pinnacle he set
> The Son of God, . . . (IV, 542-50),

with what result we know.

IV

WHAT WE HAVE BEEN describing is a flatness, a refusal to exploit space and dimension in *Paradise Regained*, even though in *Paradise Lost* space functions as a continuing metaphoric interplay with narrative. At the ideational crisis of *Paradise Lost* time becomes space; at the ideational crisis of *Paradise Regained* space becomes time. This suggests to me that there is no real temptation in *Paradise Regained*. Instead, what reader and actors alike experience is what Perry Miller has described, in connection with another great Puritan, as the endurance in time of an event which takes place outside of time: "The anxiety of living with . . . certitude, of working out the given."[17] Andrew and Simon know that "Now, now, for sure, deliverance is at hand" (II, 35), that "the time is come" (II, 43). Satan and Christ alike have heard the voice from heaven by which they "knew the time / Now full" (I, 286-7). And as the final tests begin, Christ tells Satan: "All things are best fulfill'd in their due time, . . . "Know'st thou not that my rising is thy fall . . . ?" (III, 182, 201). "Let that come when it comes," cries Satan (III, 204). The morning-star image at the opening of the poem has warned us: the time is now.[18]

If there is no temptation then, but only the exfoliation of the eternally given into time, it is organic that the focus should be inward, upon the dialectic, and that externals should reflect in their presentation the contemptuous dismissal they meet with from Christ, that they should be developed only as flat counters for ideas without sensual dimensions in a world without spatial dimensionality. If we sometimes seem to see Christ "tracing the Desert wild," we know that the real stage for the drama was revealed when he "Into himself descended" (II, 109, 111). In the shorter epic, as in the greater, we meet with Milton's insistent aesthetic principle, that form should become symbol; that style and structure should interpenetrate with narrative, not as vehicle and tenor, but in the stricter way of metaphor, by becoming "corporal," a body in which the "argument" is perceived with immediacy.

And yet, the last gesture of Satan *is* physical. We earlier looked at its crucial lines; let us now fill them in:

---

[17] Perry Miller, "John Bunyan's *Pilgrim's Progress*," in *Classics of Religious Devotion* (Boston, 1950), pp. 75-6.

[18] Gordon W. O'Brien, *Renaissance Poetics and the Problem of Power* (Chicago, 1956), pp. 9-16, discusses Renaissance concern with knowledge in "the fullness of time." William Empson, *Some Versions of Pastoral*, pp. 181-3, comments on the ambivalence Milton shows in developing the morning-star image. See below, pp. 123-4.

> To whom thus Jesus: also it is written,
> Tempt not the Lord thy God; he said and stood.
> But Satan smitten with amazement fell
> As when Earth's Son *Antæus* (to compare
> Small things with greatest) in *Irassa* strove
> With *Jove's Alcides,* and oft foil'd still rose,
> Receiving from his mother Earth new strength,
> Fresh from his fall, and fiercer grapple join'd,
> Throttl'd at length in the Air, expir'd and fell;
> So after many a foil the Tempter proud,
> Renewing fresh assaults, amidst his pride
> Fell whence he stood to see his Victor fall (IV, 560-71).

The last attempt must return us to the spatial dimension, for the Satan who attempted to rebuild heaven from the mold of hell is trapped in that space and matter to which his pride gave birth; Antaeus has at last taken a significant place in the pantheon of Christian typology.[19]

But the refrain upon "fall" as well as the adverbs in this passage also urge us through time toward finality. The fullness of time has come for Christ the man, but not yet for man. The fall has been repeated time and again through space — it is the history of evil and Providence. But as Christ stands fast against that trial which alone proves him more than man "Worth naming Son of God" (IV, 539), the poem closes, and the angels explain the deepest sense of the triumphant title and theme as they sing of how Christ:

> . . . hast regain'd lost Paradise,
> And frustrated the conquest fraudulent:
>
> .   .   .   .
>
> For though that seat of earthly bliss be fail'd,
> A fairer Paradise is founded now

[19] Cf. Frye, "Typology of *Paradise Regained*," p. 237.

For *Adam* and his chosen Sons, whom thou
A Saviour art come down to re-install,
Where they shall dwell secure, when time shall be
Of Tempter and Temptation without fear.
But thou, Infernal Serpent, shalt not long
Rule in the Clouds; like an Autumnal Star
Or Lightning thou shalt fall from Heav'n trod down
Under his feet: . . . (IV, 608-621).

In Christ's salvation of mankind this great argument will be complete, and space and time alike will be only symbols with which finitude shadows the eternal myth of the fortunate fall.

When once our heav'nly-guided soul shall climb,
Then all this Earthy grossness quit,
Attir'd with Stars, we shall forever sit,
Triumphing over Death, and Chance, and thee
O Time.

In these words Milton had in the early poem, "On Time," gathered the quintessence of his epic plot and its symbolic frame. In *Paradise Lost* and *Paradise Regained* fortune again takes the inevitable guise of space, but for Milton space asserts itself as the pawn of Providence.

IV

SCENIC STRUCTURE
IN *PARADISE LOST*

IF SPACE IS MANIPULATED as a symbolic sub
stratum, restating the "argument" by implication throughout the
course of *Paradise Lost,* it will be well for Milton's reader to bear
in mind Cassirer's demonstrations that the "development of the
mythical feeling of space always starts from the opposition of
day and *night, light* and *darkness.*"[1] It will be the argument
of this chapter that if we examine the physical structure of the
epic, the setting and movement of the narrative insofar as they
are coalescing motions through space and time, we can arrive
at a more determinate view of metaphoric structure in *Paradise
Lost* than we have been able to support to this point.[2]

---

[1] *Philosophy of Symbolic Forms,* II, 96.

[2] In an earlier chapter attention was directed to Isabel MacCaffrey's valuable
analyses of major structural factors in *Paradise Lost.* It will be clear that her
mythic approach discovered forms amenable to the patterns I have been tracing,
if we recall some typical conclusions, such as, "Milton experienced the world
of his epic architecturally, in terms of mass and space. [He employed] the
modulation of time into spatial effects" (*Paradise Lost as "Myth,"* pp. 76-7).
This critic also has important comments upon what I choose to call the "scenic
structure" of the epic: "The light of *Paradise Lost,* in mythical fashion, sums
up many . . . ideas, it is the source of life, of purity, of truth, and in itself
contains them all. It is an actor in the drama" (p. 170); "Light is related, of

It is perhaps useful to begin by reconsidering E. M. W. Till-yard's frequently-exploited decision that the "crisis" of *Paradise Lost* is not that moment in which Eve "pluckt, / She eat," but the whole of Books Nine and Ten, the disintegration and realign-

---

course, always to *one* of the two basic dimensions of *Paradise Lost,* height and depth" (p. 172; cf. the entire discussion of light imagery, pp. 169-76). Her analysis of spiritual-physical imagery is invaluable in its clarity (pp. 66-70). The self-imposed limitation of this admirable book, it seems to me, is that it is dedicated to illustrating the mythic techniques of *Paradise Lost* rather than demonstrating the sustained organization of those techniques as coherent articulation. This last is the aim of my own reading, which concurs in many conclusions with that of MacCaffrey.

It should also be noticed at this point that Josephine Miles drew attention to some particularly significant functionings of Milton's light imagery in "From Good to Bright: A Note in Poetic History," *PMLA,* LX (1945), 766-74. Briefly, she traces a poetic adjectival shift after the Elizabethan-Metaphysical heyday from a dominance of "good-bad" complexes to the "bright-dark" pattern, finding the new tradition to pivot around Milton, in whose work "descriptive detail, sensuous scenic detail became a chief material of poetry . . . for the first time in Milton it appeared consistently and abundantly enough to be recognizable as a chief qualitative factor" (p. 770).

The most important discussions of light in *Paradise Lost* between the respective publications of Miles and MacCaffrey have been the following: Don Cameron Allen, *The Harmonious Vision,* pp. 95-109; Kester Svendsen, *Milton and Science,* pp. 61-75, *et passim;* William B. Hunter, Jr., "Holy Light in 'Paradise Lost,'" *The Rice Institute Pamphlet,* XLVI (1960), 1-14; William B. Hunter, Jr., "The Meaning of Holy Light in *Paradise Lost* III," *MLN,* LXXIV (1959), 589-92. Cleanth Brooks and John Hardy elaborately, and sometimes erratically, analyzed the structural properties of light imagery in "L'Allegro—Il Penseroso" and in *Comus* (*Poems of Mr. John Milton: The 1645 Edition with Essays in Analysis,* pp. 131-44, 187-234). Rosemond Tuve is generally instructive for Miltonic critics in her analysis of light symbolism in *Comus* (*Images and Themes in Five Poems by Milton,* pp. 146-53). Other studies have been cursory, or have largely eschewed analysis for historical explanation and analogues. Among the latter, two are of particular ambitiousness, and serve at least to point up important elements of the milieu which produced *Paradise Lost.* William B. Hunter, Jr., in "Milton's Materialistic Life Principle," *JEGP,* XLV (1946), 68-76, and in "Milton and Thrice Great Hermes," *JEGP,* XLV (1946), 327-36, relates Milton to the Hermetic tradition in making the Sun the energy-emanating principle in creation, but is wholly unconvincing in his argument that Milton's souls return to the sun to await their final awakening. Walter Clyde Curry, *Milton's Ontology,* pp. 189-204, argues analogies between Milton's conception of the function of light and that found in the *Zohar.* He also considers at length the energic processes of the sun (criticizing, incidentally, Hunter's views, pp. 138-9), pp. 114-43.

ment of the relationship between Adam and Eve.[3] Tillyard finds
here what he calls the "domestication" of both crisis and epic:
"if Milton made the reconciliation of Adam and Eve his crisis
he was doing something very bold and very new. . . . Shakespeare
in the course of his Histories and Tragedies moved from an
official type of historical play to a type where people are first
and politics second. Milton in moving from the official heroic
epic to domestic life did much the same. But working in a more
solemn tradition . . . he showed the greater daring."[4] Tillyard
associates this aspect of Milton's innovation (although he carefully provides for a partial model in the *Odyssey*) with the great
impact of the Puritan epic upon the eighteenth century, where
the practical postlapsarian effort of Adam and Eve to "make life
on earth more tolerable . . . has in fact, among many others,
the Robinson Crusoe bent." This is already a movement toward
the matter of the English novel, and Tillyard concludes his
survey with Gibbon precisely because he feels that the expan-
sion in modern life after the French Revolution interred the
epic proper while transferring its characteristics to the newer
genre: "the epic spanning a total society, like Homer's or
Dante's, became impossible. Any great work of literature, however ambitious of universality, was forced to be in some degree
specialist." But the epic spirit gradually shifted to the novel
in the eighteenth century, and the nineteenth-century works
which come closest to being "epic" are domestic novels which
cut a wide swath, the *Heart of Midlothian* and *Middlemarch*.[5]

I trouble to review Tillyard's thesis because it seems to me that
he is correct in associating *Paradise Lost* with certain aspects
of modern encyclopedic form, but that a critique of his mistaken

[3] Tillyard considered the idea important enough to introduce his new stand
into the Preface to the "fourth impression" of his *Milton* (London, 1949),
p. vi. Subsequently he elaborated his argument in *Studies in Milton* (London,
1951), pp. 8-52, then restated it and drew out post-Miltonic implications in
The English Epic and Its Background (London, 1954), pp. 430-47, 528-31.
[4] *The English Epic and Its Background*, pp. 437-8.
[5] Ibid., pp. 528-31.

view of the structural properties inherent in the epic's "domesti-cation" will start us toward a sounder view. It is an error to associate the Odyssean domestication with Milton's epic, because the *Odyssey* exploits an entirely different form, the form of romance, of the quest, a form lineally expanded and therefore possessing the "crisis" development which preoccupies a criti-cism nurtured by the Aristotelian principle of the beginning, middle, and end. And our earlier analysis of the metaphoric tendencies of both modern criticism and of Milton would scarcely encourage us to expect an analogous form to dominate *Paradise Lost*. Milton's epic certainly cannot offer its richest rewards to a critic who seeks its "sequential and processive form."[6]

To select the most obvious modern version of an atemporal, nonsequential structure, we might turn attention once more to *Finnegans Wake;* in several respects, I believe, comparison with Joyce's book illuminates the form of *Paradise Lost*. We may first observe a profound commonplace: both works are composed in the manner of a painting. I do not mean, of course, that they reveal a descriptive surface which is reflective of paintings, in the way of those critics who have (often quite usefully) applied the *ut pictura poesis* formula to *The Faerie Queene* or have discussed "baroque" elements in Milton's work. Rather, I mean that these books have been meticulously structured, as a painting is quite naturally constructed, utilizing spatial line (the basic movement upward and downward within a given area) and the interplay of light and dark tones as both the formal and the meaning pattern. In short, I suggest that in these elements meta-phoric tenor and vehicle merge, an inevitable process in painting, where the artist must visually express a theme which cannot be

[6] I quote the phrase from Northrop Frye's description of the "quest" myth. In his discussion of this pattern, Frye embraces both *Paradise Lost* and *Finnegans Wake,* but by making the quest-form merge with a cyclical shape, he also embraces both Tillyard's definition of form in *Paradise Lost* and my own. This seems to me a debilitating fusion for practical criticism (see *Anatomy of Criticism*, pp. 186-96, 313-26).

discursively appropriated to the form, but a distinctively rare achievement in longer literary works.

To pursue this point, we may observe that *Finnegans Wake* is the history of a night world, of a dreamer moving through midnight terrors and guilt into morning, while *Paradise Lost* is a world of emanating light, "Light from above, from the fountain of light," which trickles away into the palpable darkness of hell. Now the painter uses light and shade as focus, the Christian as almost inevitable symbol (recalling the impasse to which it brought religious discourse in the seventeenth century, tragically inevitable), and mankind as the image of its deepest impulses; the artist can choose to use them in the three functions simultaneously. When he does so, he not only possesses his work of a basic formal pattern, but he also makes it capable of automatically calling up a rich variety of psychological and literary associations.

Further, both works under comparison obtain a primary structure by expanding the metaphoric definition of their mutual theme, a fall and subsequent arising and resurrection, into literal movement, once again merging a central tenor and vehicle in such a way that scene continually acts as mimesis of argument. It will be observed that this is antithetical to the primarily horizontal movement of the "quest" narrative, of the *Odyssey* or of Joyce's earlier *Ulysses,* which directs both structure and theme into the road of search, the long line which is Western culture's natural psychological symbol for the passage of time, the processive.

This vertical spatial organization of Milton's epic is complicated by the circular development of the narrative, which does, of course, have its temporal aspect (how this temporal aspect is consistently subsumed by the spatial dimension was the argument of the preceding chapter). The stage of heaven-earth-hell is set in motion by the circle in which eternity encompasses history, all things happening at once as God looks upon time as a place, which the poet describes as God himself might: non-sequentially narrating the swing from the beginning of history at the first fall to the end of history at the last resurrection. The poem moves in scene and narration, then, on a vertical axis swinging in a great circle.[7] It is just so with *Finnegans Wake*, where the last line of the narrative completes the first, where the wake is prelude to an awakening and resurrection. Neither work, in fact, has a center from which one might measure the distances relating beginning, middle, end or "crisis"; in this they are diametrically different from the poem Tillyard describes. But given this centerless structure, we can see that the "domestication" of the epic of man or of Here Comes Everybody provides precisely the only structure through which the poet *can* organically draw all of a complex culture into a pattern of meaningful relationships. The "plot" of the narrative is an unmistakable symbol of the cyclical rhythms of rise and fall which is not only the myth of man's history but the reification of his individual domestic, physical, sexual, and spiritual experience. This implies, however, that the characters moving in such a structure will act as microcosms, metaphors for man's filial mimesis of the rhythms of nature. The particular protagonist, precisely because he is "domesticated" in this sense, absorbs into his microcosmic story all of the disparate cultural elements which the poet is capable of injecting into his narrative through the cumulatively thickening associations of metaphor, double plot, allusion or simile. The protagonist, in sum, possesses for his mirror image an infinitely usable macrocosm which can be indefinitely expanded without upsetting the balance of the aesthetic structure.[8]

[7] It may be appropriate to say that my formulation seems incompatible with the "circular" structuring of the epic discerned by M. M. Mahood, *Poetry and Humanism* (London, 1950), pp. 177-87.

[8] MacCaffrey, *Paradise Lost as "Myth,"* pp. 45-52, presents a structural description in some respects paralleling my own, although I do not thoroughly understand her image of a "spiral."

Allusiveness constitutes one of the chief aesthetic dimensions of *Paradise Lost,* and the discovery of allusion and analogue was the major task to which Miltonic critics addressed themselves from the eighteenth century until the recent intensified interest which we have noticed. It is no derogation of Milton's artistic awareness to assert that the areas of allusiveness in many cases were not available to the poet's consciousness of particulars but derive legitimacy from the structural elements of the poem as I have tried to describe them.

It may be instructive to consider a Shakespearean instance which is both parallel and antipodal in effect. In recent years, two readers have independently traced the persistent imagistic and stage patterns of rising and falling in *Richard II* and together demonstrate impressively how this element threads throughout the drama.[9] And yet, the effect is immensely different because the protagonists are *not* microcosmic, but regal, and the struggle limited insofar as the kneeling and descending speeches and scenes call up the literature of the Fall of Princes, or — at the furthest reach — the Wheel of Fortune. Rich as they are, such traditions cannot seek analogues universally, but constitute an area in which Shakespeare undoubtedly controlled his audience in large part consciously, as a matter of particular intention (I am not unaware of the dangerous paradoxes in the term). But when one "domesticates" H. C. Earwicker, whose name is also Adam, in a context which does not employ, but rather is structured from, metaphors of the profoundest cultural enrichment, there can be no question of conscious limitations enforced by the poet; there can, indeed, be no question of limitations at all: the poem continues to subsume the myths of the future into its own structure, a metaphoric circle without center. This, I take it, is what makes a poem "universal" in scope. I take it, too, that

[9] Paul A. Jorgensen, "Vertical Patterns in *Richard II*," *SAB,* XXIII (1948), 119-34, and Arthur Suzman, "Imagery and Symbolism in *Richard II*," *SQ,* VII (1956), 355-70.

this is the ideal version of the modern mythographic artist's spatial form which Frank analyzed so effectively. Its impact is always incalculable. If we recall Joyce's *Ulysses,* it should not be hard to agree that the sequential "quest" movement, which is apparent as skeleton, is overpowered so strongly by the atemporal "mythic" juxtapositions that the novel is usually considered to exhibit a natural structural kinship with *Finnegans Wake.*

One might at first glance argue that Adam is, after all, *not* HCE or Everyman, but stands in peculiar isolation from his fallen heirs throughout a poem of paradise. But it is through the consistently metaphoric nature of the scenes in heaven, hell and paradise alike, that we are made from the beginning affectively aware of his humanity; this metaphoric scene is a structure which transcends narrative to persuade us of our common dilemma with the first father of us all. For if the general structural mode is inevitably effective, Milton's choice of light and dark, descent and ascent as his primary dimensions is the factor which allows him to transcend all the limitations of relevance which narrative normally imposes, as in the cases of *Richard II* or the Wandering Jew, Leopold Bloom. Enough has been said about light and darkness without invoking the history of Christian, Manichaean or Platonic traditions. Second only to this traditional symbolism in historical and psychic layers of association, however, is the pattern of fall and resurrection. It is, of course, the very essence of religious mythology, emphatic in the Ovidian and Hesiodic geneses as in that of Christianity. The *felix culpa* as Fortunate fall[10] is the mystery

---

[10] Cf. Arthur O. Lovejoy, "Milton and the Paradox of the Fortunate Fall," *ELH,* IV (1937), 161-79. I am not convinced by the interesting argument that "Milton did not believe in a Fortunate Fall and was in no wise proposing the idea in *Paradise Lost*" proposed in Dick Taylor, Jr., "Milton and the Paradox of the Fortunate Fall Once More," *Tulane Studies in English,* IX (1959), 35-51. His argument might be applicable to any orthodox Christian theologian, but seems particularly unsuccessful in interpreting Adam's last speech and God's lament for Man (XI, 84-98). Similar argument, less fully developed,

of the phoenix rising from its ashes; of Proserpina returning more poignantly to day because of the long night of the underworld; of nature's rhythm of seeding and rising out of the earth which lies behind Proserpina's myth. And it is also the image for the closely related experience of man's own sexual rhythms.

Since the Christian myth finds its central meaning in the projection of a mythic fall and resurrection into spiritual metaphor, and since the Hebraic origins inextricably interlaced Christian myth with the language and milieu of pastoral,[11] the choice of sexuality as the chief image of evil at crucial points in *Paradise Lost* was no personal nor merely traditional accident, but perhaps the most important single stroke of unifying genius in the epic, a remark I will attempt to clarify in relation to my general remarks upon the scenic structure.

Sex is, of course, the principal traditional focus for sensuality, and as such has always been deeply embedded in the guilt sense of Christian culture. It is also that microcosmic version of the fall which is most thoroughly realized by every man, as well as that which is best calculated to open out toward speculation on the nature of permanence and change. But perhaps the significance of sexuality in *Paradise Lost* is best approached through recalling what it might have been but was not. The physically elaborated conception of Christ as the spouse of the love-thirsting soul, so popular in the Catholic and Anglican traditions, confronted Milton in the writings of St. Teresa, Marino, and their Cambridge followers, Richard Crashaw and Joseph Beaumont, and it was a tradition not without echoes in

---

has been presented in H. V. S. Ogden, "The Crisis of *Paradise Lost* Reconsidered," *PQ*, XXXVI (1957), 17-9. Cf., in contrast, the recent strengthening of Lovejoy's case in William G. Madsen, "The Fortunate Fall in *Paradise Lost*," *MLN*, LXXIV (1959), 103-5. Broadbent, *Some Graver Subject*, pp. 248, 253, 282-6, finds the *felix culpa* motif in the poem, but also finds that inherently it possesses "little poetic force."

[11] Rosemond Tuve has some excellent observations on the matter in relation to "Lycidas" (*Images and Themes in Five Poems by Milton*, pp. 81-7).

Donne and George Herbert. In this context, sex is the achievement of union: one "dies" with connotations startlingly similar to those in the bawdy poems of Donne or Dryden or Rochester. There is a swooning away in the consummation of a pleasing pain from which one revives. But where the wits revive to die again, Beaumont's Psyche moves beyond our vision into the glorious embrace of paradise. The sexual imagery has made the paradise a passionately physical one, and the powerful effects of religious ecstasy are in danger of becoming either mere sensationalism or sentimentality. It is a way which can be exploited greatly, but always at a sacrifice. For its exoticism creates a distancing, an estrangement even, between our own reticences and normal associations and the lushly physical imaging of religious paradox. There is no suggestion of this in *Paradise Lost*; Christ is the son, never even potentially the spouse.[12]

Indeed, when sexuality enters the poem, it enters as Sin (II, 750-809). If Bunyan's Christian is impressive with his great burden on his back, the nice realization of the allegory pales beside the rightness of Milton's description of Sin coming to birth as an ambivalently welcomed siren, and the growth of our burden within, not without, as Bunyan in his particular literalism and honesty perceived it. Then the burden tumbles forth as Death, dropped from the womb of Sin fallen with Satan; and the emphasis is upon return as he falls upon his mother to bring into the world a proliferous demonic breed which balances God's "new Race call'd *Man*." And these return again and again to gnaw the dark and vicious place whence they came, even as man will return when time is past into the "holy Light" of God which conceived him, too, when, as Milton cries, Thou "satst

---

[12] A point very similar is implied in Malcolm Ross, *Poetry and Dogma: The Transfiguration of Eucharistic Symbols in Seventeenth-Century English Poetry* (New Brunswick, 1954), pp. 218-23 *et passim.* Further, this seems a function of the poem rather than of the poet. E. M. W. Tillyard pointed out long ago the "religious eroticism" which marks the close of the *Epitaphium Damonis* (*Milton*, pp. 382-3).

brooding on the vast Abyss / And mad'st it pregnant" (I, 21-22). We should know even now that sex and sin endlessly repeating the process must catch man up in the cycle. And since sex is a creative act, we should see that it is the only possible symbol for that jealousy of the Creator which hurtled Satan downward. And, finally, we should understand why there is no suggestion of Christ the spouse in *Paradise Lost,* no touch of the religious sexuality so marked in Milton's milieu as to be flirted with even in the language of many Puritans.[13] For Sin tells Satan, "Thyself in me thy perfect image viewing / Becam'st enamour'd (II, 764-5). He loves her as God loves his image in the creation, and this is the first bitter parody, the first act of imperfection and negation of God's order. For Satan has made a material idol, not as yet in historical, but in aesthetic, fact. Sin will become historically realized and begin to give birth when her own birth has activated the fall of Satan which, in turn, activates the making of matter (for if matter is made for God's glory, it is made through Satan's instrumentality as an apparent cause). And sexuality will be the obscene, awkward means by which Satan and the material world can ape God's creative fiat. As Adam's last vision implies, sexuality and sin will join with matter in a rhythm of lust and destructiveness, rising repeatedly to populate the earth in the acts of Satan and Eve.

But this confronts us with Adam and Eve. Their sexuality is condoned in the bower scenes of Book IV; and yet this, like the eternal stability of spring in a garden of plenitude where without effort things grow too fast, is an unrealizable symbol of innocence. The breeding and multiplying of nature and of man are at one level God's reaction to Satan's active seduction of and by Sin; and, like nature's seasonal cycles, like the matter of the world itself, the sexual act is patterned into the inevitable but

[13] Cf. V. De Sola Pinto, "Libertines and Puritans: A Note on Some Lyrics of the Late Seventeenth and Early Eighteenth Centuries," *N&Q,* CCV (1960), 224-6, and Broadbent, *Some Graver Subject,* pp. 60-2.

not yet unfolded imperfection of the fallen world created in consequence of the first fall. Thus, we should not be surprised that Satan's sin is given imagistic expression as a type for Adam's own inordinate love of woman; nor that the first stimulus of the death fruit will be to lascivious sexuality; nor that the first shame will be the shame of sexuality.[14]

And yet, all is not negative. That prophecy which dominates both *Paradise Lost* and *Paradise Regained*, the bruising of the serpent by "the seed," predicates the ultimate intention of God to turn even this central symbol of evil to greater good: if Sin introduces evil into the world as sexuality, God will make it the instrument for repopulating heaven with the seed of saints, and woman will bring forth that man who will harrow hell and send Satan spinning to his ultimate fall. Through the flesh the flesh will be transcended.

> As with new Wine intoxicated both
> They swim in mirth, and fancy that they feel
> Divinity within them breeding wings
> Wherewith to scorn the Earth:[15] but that false Fruit
> Far other operation first display'd,
> Carnal desire inflaming, . . .
>
> .   .   .   .
>
> Her hand he seiz'd, and to a shady bank,
> Thick overhead with verdant roof imbowr'd
> He led her nothing loath; Flow'rs were the Couch,

[14] Svendsen, *Milton and Science*, pp. 165-70, analyzes the phallic implications of the serpent, both in tradition and in the description of Eve's tempter (*PL*, IX, 494-510); cf. W. B. C. Watkins, *An Anatomy of Milton's Verse* (Baton Rouge, 1955), pp. 126-46; J. B. Broadbent, "Milton's Hell," *ELH*, XXI (1954), 173-6.

[15] Sin at the fall tightens her bond of parallel with Eve when through "sympathy, or some connatural force" she feels "new strength within me rise, / Wings growing and Dominion giv'n me large / Beyond this Deep" (X, 243-7); cf. Rajan, *Paradise Lost and the Seventeenth Century Reader*, pp. 44-5.

> Pansies, and Violets, and Asphodel,
> And Hyacinth, Earth's freshest softest lap.
> There they thir fill of Love and Love's disport
> Took largely, of thir mutual guilt the Seal,
> The solace of thir sin, till dewy sleep
> Oppress'd them, wearied with thir amorous play (IX, 1008-1045).

In the antithesis between expectation and the act, Milton plays jauntily as an obscene joker upon the physical aspect of sex as a "fall." But the fall of the lascivious first parents is upon a couch of flowers, just as the simile makes the sexual act of unfallen Adam and Eve in the heart of their bower an analogue to spring fertility:

> . . . half her swelling Breast
> Naked met his under the flowing Gold
> Of her loose tresses hid: he in delight
> Both of her Beauty and submissive Charms
> Smil'd with superior Love, as *Jupiter*
> On *Juno* smiles, when he impregns the Clouds
> That shed *May* flowers . . . (IV, 495-501).

For sex is the creative force of seasonal change in this lost world; but that seasonal change is glorified as imitation of God's original creation catalogued in Book VII, and softened through constant involvement with the universal garden of pastoral tradition. Winter threatens a world of spring, but, as Proserpina reminds us, winter itself promises rebirth. And it is the rebirth of a world *rising*, even as "out of the ground up rose / As from his Lair the wild Beast" (VII, 456-7) in the original creation. Sex, then, is the symbol of death, but of death as it fits into the paradoxical fortunate-fall pattern of the poem: a dying fall into renewed life, the death of a world which never ceases until "The World shall burn, and from her ashes spring / New Heav'n and Earth" (III, 334-5).[16]

The theme of renewal, however, is inextricably bound to the other primary structural pattern of contrast and alternation between light and dark. Later we will explore how thoroughly and literally Milton's petitions to his muse for an inner light, that he "may see and tell / Of things invisible to mortal sight" (III, 54-5), are developed in contrast with physical blindness. The point need not be stressed here, except to observe that the inverse proportioning of physical sight to spiritual insight experienced by the poet-prophet is drawn into rapport with the symbolism of the narrative proper when the same inversions are exierenced by Adam and Eve during the course of their fall and recovery.

Adam, having debated with God the need for a companion, is "strain'd to the highth" by the effort and "Dazzl'd and spent, sunk down, and sought repair / Of sleep, which instantly fell" (VIII, 454-8). This is no ordinary sleep, but a sinking into vision from the borders of the perceptible. Adam proceeds to recount for Raphael God's manner of preparing him for the creation of Eve:

> Mine eyes he clos'd, but op'n left the Cell
> Of Fancy my internal sight, by which
> Abstract as in a trance, methought I saw

the emergence of Eve from the rib wound. But when her sweetness had been formed and Adam enamored, "Shee disappear'd, and left me dark, I wak'd / To find her" (VIII, 460-79).[17]

---

[16] Watkins, *An Anatomy of Milton's Verse*, pp. 42-86, has perceptively explored the ambivalence toward sex in the imagery of *Paradise Lost*. For a traditional negative view, see C. S. Lewis, *A Preface to Paradise Lost*, pp. 118-20.

[17] The context of sensuality and uxoriousness which leads Adam to admit to the angelic counselor, "here passion first I felt" (530), or "All higher knowledge in her presence falls" (551), reminds us that Adam, like Satan,

After the sexual "fall" of the mortal afternoon, as the first
parents awoke from troubled slumber, the pattern of vision had
been inverted; they:

> Soon found thir Eyes how op'n'd, and thir minds
> How dark'n'd; innocence, that as a veil
> Had shadow'd them from knowing ill, was gone (IX, 1053-5).

The phrasing reminds us that this is ironic fulfillment of Satan's
prophecy during the temptation of Eve, when he assured her
that God:

> . . . knows that in the day
> Ye Eat thereof, your Eyes that seem so clear,
> Yet are but dim, shall perfectly be then
> Op'n'd and clear'd, and ye shall be as Gods,
> Knowing both Good and Evil as they know (IX, 705-9).

Eve had passed on the argument to Adam in her persuasions
toward joining in sin, asserting that the fruit was "of Divine
effect / To open Eyes" because she now found "opener mine
Eyes, / Dim erst" (IX, 865-6; 875-6; cf. the later 985). Adam
at the awakening picks up the prophecy of the fiend that lied
like truth with grim ironic discovery: "true in our Fall, / False
in our promis'd Rising; since our Eyes / Op'n'd we find indeed"
(IX, 1069-71).

But Adam, first to fall on evil days and dark, will learn, like
the poet who is his creator and type, the bittersweet lesson of

---

is "idolatrous" of his own image in Eve, and may be associated with an earlier
vision of idolatrous sensuality to which Milton adds nonscriptural emphases:
> . . . the Love-tale
> Infected *Sion's* daughters with like heat,
> Whose wanton passions in the sacred Porch
> *Ezekial* saw, when by the Vision led
> His eye survey'd the dark Idolatries
> Of alienated *Judah* (I, 452-7).

obedience and hope. He will learn, like Milton, through that blindness which is the outward face of the inner vision of prophecy. On the hilltop from which Adam is about to see the history of his seed and learn the paradox of the fortunate fall:

> *Michael* from *Adam's* eyes the Film remov'd
> Which that false Fruit that promis'd clearer sight
> Had bred; then purg'd with Euphrasy and Rue
> The visual Nerve, for he had much to see;
> And from the Well of Life three drops instill'd.
> So deep the power of these Ingredients pierc'd,
> Ev'n to the inmost seat of mental sight,
> That *Adam* now enforc't to close his eyes,
> Sunk down and all his Spirits became intranst (XI, 412-20).

And at the close of the vision and narration, Adam cries out in the same terms:

> . . . O sent from Heav'n,
> Enlight'ner of my darkness, gracious things
> Thou hast reveal'd . . .
> . . . now first I find
> Mine eyes true op'ning, . . .
> .   .   .   .
> . . . but now I see
> His day. . . . (XII, 270-7).

In these instances, in spite of the couch of flowers, the love sleep, or Adam's ascension of the mount, the light and dark imagery becomes symbolic in conjunction with a fall and resurrection which may affect us as conceptualized metaphors, so thoroughly absorbed through transference to the spiritual realm, that it is perverse to insist that the reader recognize their literal resonances. And, indeed, it is true that our being conscious of these echoes at all is a function of the total poem, in which, from the first, light and dark have been relevant to physical as well as spiritual place.[18] Heaven is light, hell is darkness. This pendent world, modeled on heaven, is a place of alternation between night and day, but the alternation is the grateful vicissitude of dimming and brightening light; only in hell is there "No light, but rather darkness visible" (I, 63).[19] It will be the demonstration of how thoroughly this pattern controls the movement of the poem from first lines to last which will, I hope, give significance to my following remarks. But it is well to recall at the outset that Milton himself is explicit about the technique by which literal and conceptual interact and merge into an organic Janus-faced symbolism. He is explicit when

[18] In addition to MacCaffrey's study, discussed above, several critics have commented relevantly upon the light and dark of *Paradise Lost* in contexts primarily concerned with the principle of contrast and movement in the epic's economy. H. V. S. Ogden, "The Principles of Variety and Contrast in Seventeenth Century Aesthetics, and Milton's Poetry," *JHI*, X (1949), 159-82, demonstrates that theorists as well as poets and painters were turning from exuberant variety toward the contrast which emerged from and revealed nature's *discordia concors*. He satisfies one that Milton consciously thought in these terms, but does not adequately analyze contrast at work in the poetry. Stein briefly comments on the "reconciliation" of light and dark in the Garden's prelapsarian state (*Answerable Style*, pp. 63-7), a point analogous to Joseph Summers' more thorough analysis of the Morning Hymn, in which he finds the epitome of the poem to be the "double motions" by which God advances his ends through oppositions ("'Grateful Vicissitude' in *Paradise Lost*," *PMLA*, LXIX [1954], 251-64). This is an imagistic version of the Dionysian-Apollonian reading of the Satan-Christ relation made by Robert Allen Durr, "Dramatic Pattern in *Paradise Lost*," *JAAC*, XIII (1955), 520-6.

[19] Fisher, "Milton's Theodicy," p. 38, comments in puzzlement upon Milton's use of darkness in *Paradise Lost* "to symbolize the negation of light and order," because in *De doctrina* "it is specifically stated that darkness is not a negation." Milton in the treatise declared: "That this darkness was far from being a mere negation, is clear from Isa. xlv.7. 'I am Jehovah; I form the light, and create darkness.' If the darkness be nothing, God in creating darkness, created nothing, . . . which is a contradiction" (*CE*, XV, 17). Here is another instance to demonstrate that while light as spiritual metaphor was unmanageable in discursive exposition, it was perfectly amenable to the metaphoric nature of poetry. On this matter, Milton probably was neither indecisive nor Manichaean; he was a poet.

Satan's forces advance with their newly-invented cannon to the second day of battle in heaven. The weapon has been manufactured in the dark night, a darkness which merges with reminiscence of the abyss when "his devilish Enginry" advances "impal'd / On every side wtih shadowing Squadrons Deep" (VI, 554-5). Satan loudly addresses his troops with instructions the military import of which will soon be understood:

> Vanguard, to Right and Left the Front unfold;
> That all may see who hate us, how we seek
> Peace and composure, and with open breast
> Stand ready to receive them, if they like
> Our overture, and turn not back perverse;
>
> .   .   .   .
> . . . while we discharge
> Freely our part: yee who appointed stand
> Do as you have in charge, and briefly touch
> What we propound, and loud that all may hear.

Before the fuses are touched, Milton comments on Satan's "scoffing in ambiguous words" (558-68). It is of course, a procedure closely allied to what Thomas Wilson had titled in English "the ambiguitie," "when the construccion bringeth error, hauing diuerse understandinges in it. . . . when sentences be spoken doubtfully, that thei maie be construed twoo maner of waies."[20]

Here, as in the passages on the fall in connection with blindness, the conceptual dominates the surface attention, while the physical makes underground connections with things past and things to come. But at least as often in the course of the poem, the proportions are to be reversed, and scene stands in sharp

---

[20] Thomas Wilson, *The Rule of Reason, conteining the Arte of Logicke* (London, 1563), fol. 66v.

outline, while around it the "argument" peers imminent but shaded.

Let us recall as an interesting test case, a specific motif. Operative at many points is what I should like to call the microcosmic fall. In these instances, the terms of the fall are utilized as sheer vehicular expression of action or idea, but inevitably throw the episode into the focus of the entire *felix culpa* development. On the level of pure narrative, we find the beginning of retribution for Satan so imaged in the description of Abdiel's first act of war in heaven: "a noble stroke he lifted high, / Which hung not, but . . . swift with tempest fell / On the proud Crest of *Satan*" (VI, 189-91). One can scarcely ignore the climactic position of the critical words, "high" and "fell," and one having progressed from the abyss to heaven can scarcely fail to realize that the fall is beginning to be re-enacted. Satan himself does not so realize, however, and therefore in the first day of battle when all is equal between angelic foes, he views the battlefield prowess of his own troops with a simplicity ironic in arousing the profound conceptual roots his words have buried in the poem: "Hast thou [Michael is addressed] turn'd the least of these / To flight, or if to fall, but that they rise / Unvanquisht" (VI, 284-6). He sees a physical equality; we have been exposed to the spiritual inequality which permits us a Sophoclean *frisson* on overhearing his boast. Raphael's version is less distinct; when closing his warning against "vain philosophy," he suggests to an Adam whose sin of knowledge is imminent:

> . . . from this high pitch let us descend
> A lower flight, and speak of things at hand
> Useful, whence haply mention may arise
> Of something not unseasonable to ask (VIII, 198-201).

But when Adam proceeds to describe Eve, the entire narrative pattern seems to leap responsive to his one sentence of terrible simplicity: "All higher knowledge in her presence falls" (VIII, 551).[21]

But nowhere is the symbolic use of light merged more faithfully with the vertical movements of the poem, nowhere is the simultaneously physical and psychic nature of the fall more carefully suggested, than in the opening of the narrative which introduces Satan on the lake and plains of hell. It should be observed as preliminary that we are made acutely aware of spatial movement by the unceasing restlessness of perspective in the first lines. As Satan was by "the Almighty Power / Hurl'd headlong flaming from th' Ethereal Sky," we watch the tremendous fall from some vantage point far out in space, but we are drawn into the picture itself with jolting suddenness to look out across the new horizon of hell through the eyes of Satan himself. Standing aside within earshot, we find ourselves listening to the first private oration to Beelzebub, but as we hear him complete the speech, our knowledge of his contradictory inner reaction reminds us that perspective, like symbols, is intertwining the outward and the inner, the physical scene and the psychically experienced. And so throughout the description: we move away to see Satan's arising from the lake; we move far out from the scene once more to watch the myriad troops draw themselves together; we find ourselves as suddenly gazing across their gathered might through Satan's eyes. Such leaping juxtapositions in perspective will not recur until Book Six — in the description of the war in heaven which was the beginning of evil from which these fallen warriors of the First Book toppled.

But the basic pattern of movement is consistently vertical, the pattern of Book One an epitome of the whole epic, a fall which

---

[21] Rajan, *Paradise Lost and the Seventeenth Century Reader,* p. 44, notes briefly the ambiguities of the word "high" in relation to Eve. Such patternings illuminate what seem to A. J. A. Waldock to be "elementary lapses" (*Paradise Lost and its Critics* [Cambridge, 1947], pp. 111-2).

concludes with a resurgence; and this ironic epitome itself is miniatured in the personal fall and arising of Satan within the embrace of the two larger patterns of book and epic. We may say that here is Satan's first and most ironic parody of the ways of God: that he, too, in rising from a fall, out of all this evil brings forth his own good, brings forth light out of darkness. The opening is not easy. The directive is given with the climactic emphasis upon the single word of spatial orientation, "down." Later we learn of a nine days' fall; here we learn only of the diabolical coma, but so presented as to merge into the description of the fall and to emphatically wed it to the light patterns. We realize that "Nine times the Space that measures Day and Night / To mortal men" (I. 50-1) is the classic proof text for Cassirer's earlier-mentioned axiom that "development of the mythical feeling of space always starts from the opposition of *day* and *night, light* and *darkness.*" I have already commented upon the concomitancy of unconfined perspectives and evil: but as Satan views "as far as Angels ken," the emphasis is less upon distance than inverted light,

> . . . on all sides round
> As one great Furnace flam'd, yet from those flames
> No light, but rather darkness visible . . . (I, 61-3).

This very darkness is utilized as a reminder of the fall through incalculable spatial distances, however, when, as so often throughout the first books, we are recalled to the spiritual antipodes mirrored in luminosity:

> . . . here their Prison ordained
> In utter darkness, and thir portion set
> As far remov'd from God and light of Heav'n
> As from the Center thrice to th' utmost Pole (I, 71-4).

The day-night, light-dark dichotomy, nonetheless, is here schematic, scarcely realized yet but as symbol, and certainly over-shadowed in effect by the geography of fire. Within thirty lines we hear of him "Hurl'd headlong flaming," of "combustion," "penal Fire," a "fiery Gulf," "Furnace flam'd," "flames," "a fiery Deluge," and "ever-burning Sulphur." When Satan turns to speak to Beelzebub, he echoes the narrator's own contrast be-tween heaven and hell in the dual terms of space and light:

> If thou beest he; but O how fall'n! how chang'd
> From him, who in the happy realms of Light
> Cloth'd with transcendent brightness didst outshine
> Myriads though bright . . .
> . . . into what Pit thou seest
> From what highth fall'n . . . (I, 84-92).

But as he goes on to speak of his own unshakeable determina-tion, of the "fierce contention" he made against God, and to boast "That Glory never shall his wrath or might / Extort from me" (110-1), we become aware that the flames are them-selves part of the over-all complexity of the light pattern, that they *are* not only Satan's "fierceness" but his "glory."

It is Sin who will tell us of her own birth, in an emblemlike tableau of, precisely, flaming darkness:

> . . . dim thine eyes, and dizzy swum
> In darkness, while thy head flames thick and fast
> Threw forth, till on the left side op'ning wide,
> Likest to thee in shape and count'nance bright,
> Then shining heav'nly fair, a Goddess arm'd
> Out of thy head I sprung . . . (II, 753-8).

In falling, Satan's original glory dims, his light takes on the eery shadows of his burning heart, strange flames that he passes

on to Sin in her birth, that darken the vault of heaven during
the course of his war against Light, and that he carries with
him into hell. "Myself am Hell": but if hell is projected from
the heart into literal landscape, that landscape is also realized as
symbol.[22] The fall from Light into hell as Satan describes it to
Beelzebub begins literally, but gradually merges literal with
metaphoric. "Merit," claims Satan, "with the mightiest *rais'd*
me to contend," and now to bow to God "were low indeed, / . . .
ignominy and shame beneath / This downfall" (I, 98-116).
And at the close, the literal has been internalized, as Satan
beneath his "vaunting" probes the bottomless consciousness of
hopeless loss, "rackt with deep despair."[23]

Nor can we fail to notice that if Sin sprang forth with the
arms which presage war in heaven, her birth interacts with

[22] The flames, too, of course, are ultimately a parody of God. Satan has
seen God speak "as from a flaming Mount, whose top / Brightness had made
invisible" (V, 598-9). When he begins the seduction of the angels, Satan
imitates this vision on "his Royal seat / High on a Hill, far blazing, as a
Mount / Rais'd on a Mount" (V, 756-8). Now the parody has been completed by inversion. Where God's flames gave off "brightness . . . invisible,"
Satan's create "darkness visible." This early inversion prepares for the contrasting parallelism of Satanic hatred and God's "reluctant flames, the sign
/ Of wrath awak't" (VI, 58-9), or the climactic image of merciful justice,
the flaming sword at Paradise gate (XI, 120-1; XII, 592, 633, 643). Man
lives in both worlds. If the fall affected him by "Carnal desire inflaming"
(IX, 1013), he will later harness fire not only to meet the physical cold
and dark of postlapsarian nature jarred, but in symbolic gesture of his will
to "add / Deeds to thy knowledge answerable" (XII, 581-2) of Grace:
        . . . such Fire to use,
    And what may else be remedy or cure
    To evils which our own misdeeds have wrought,
    Hee will instruct us praying, and of Grace
    Beseeching him, . . . (X, 1078-82).
Cf. MacCaffrey, *Paradise Lost as "Myth,"* pp. 160-4, for other cogent observations on fire symbolism. She clearly errs, however, in stating that "Fire,
its products, and its powers, are alike 'guilty' in *Paradise Lost*" (p. 161).

[23] Joseph E. Duncan, "Milton's Four-in-One-Hell," *HLQ*, XX (1957),
127-36, has some comments upon the interplay of physical and psychic in
the description of hell, as does Ernest Schanzer, "Milton's Hell Revisited,"
UTQ, XXIV (1955), 136-45. Both are rather casual, however, and the
definitive statement of Milton's mode of conception and its tradition is
Merritt Y. Hughes, "Myself Am Hell," *MP*, LIV (1956), 80-95.

the light pattern of the poem in other ways besides providing the original milieu of flames; for it is certainly another irony upon Satan's promise to Eve in the temptation, another parody upon the holy blindness of Man and poet, that Sin should remind Satan how "dim his eyes" as she came into flaming being.

This is only the first complication, a second soon follows. Addressing his cohort, Satan concludes by looking at the darkness lit only by his own fire of Sin: "Seest thou yon dreary Plain . . . void of light, / Save what the glimmering of these livid flames / Casts pale and dreadful? Thither let us tend" (I, 180-4). So urging, Satan rises from darkness into flight, and as he ascends, Milton lavishes attention upon a miniature of his total structure, the angel beginning immediately to show remnants of his quondam glory. His "Eyes . . . sparkling blaz'd" (193-4), his shield "Hung on his shoulders like the Moon" (287). Satan's brilliance, of course, like that of the moon, is as derivative and misleading as his rhetoric, a condition implied by the first epic simile, inserted at that moment in which he arises from the burning flood:

Thus Satan . . .

.   .   .   .

Lay floating many a rood, in bulk as huge
As whom the Fables name of monstrous size,

.   .   .   .

Leviathan, which God of all his works
Created hugest that swim th' Ocean stream:
Him haply slumb'ring on the *Norway* foam
The Pilot of some small night-founder'd Skiff,
Deeming some Island, oft, as Seamen tell,
With fixed Anchor in his scaly rind
Moors by his side under the Lee, while Night
Invests the Sea, and wished Morn delays (192-208).

Not only is Satan imaged in one of his scriptural types, but even as he is rising out of darkness he is made the symbol of night, the attractive seducer "to his own dark designs" (213) who will whisper to Eve in the first unquiet midnight in the history of paradise, so that when she awakens she will cry to Adam in echo of the betrayed seamen, "glad I see / Thy face, and Morn return'd" (V, 29-30).

This simile of the darkly bulking Leviathan is our notice that the cycle has begun. Satan fallen has rearisen, with the "high permission of all-ruling Heaven" (I, 212), that Man may fall to rise again into new life even while Satan himself is hurtling back into the dark pit of oblivion:

> . . . all his malice serv'd but to bring forth
> Infinite goodness, grace and mercy shown
> On Man by him seduc't, but on himself
> Treble confusion, wrath and vengeance pour'd (I, 217-20).

But the paradox is not only stated explicitly; it is enacted in puns of hope throughout the description of Satan's ascent, puns which deepen the evolving sense of light and dark symbolism. As Satan rises with sparkles of his old light, it is upon the "*dusky* Air" but on "dry Land / He *lights*" (I, 226-8: my italics). It is Milton's pun, and Satan seems aware of it, as a moment later he counterpoints humor with poignant remorse: "Is this the Region, . . . this the seat / That we must change for Heav'n, this mournful gloom / For that celestial light?" (242-5). But it is Beelzebub who immediately thereafter perpetrates the cruelest pun of all in addressing Satan as "Leader of those Armies bright, / Which but th' Omnipotent none could have foiled" (272-3). When the rebel armies at last rise from the burning marl, it is in the traditional image of the plague of locusts, and hence they rise from dark to dark, themselves hell, "a pitchy cloud / Of *Locusts* . . . Like Night, . . . darken'd all the Land" until "in even balance down they light" (338-50).

However, it *is* the period of diabolic ascent, so that these promising inversions of the light and dark as measures of the vertical scale can be only minor notes, shadowings of the great paradox in which the action moves. Consequently, the larger structure is obedient to the basic symbolic direction, and as Satan's troops rise before their overlord, their remaining brilliance shoots upward into the reaches beyond hell to join with that light whence they were derived:

> *Azazel* at his right, a Cherub tall:
> Who forthwith from the glittering Staff unfurl'd
> Th' Imperial Ensign, which full high advanc't
> Shone like a Meteor streaming to the Wind
> With Gems and Golden lustre rich imblaz'd,
> Seraphic arms and Trophies: all the while
> Sonorous metal blowing Martial sounds:
> At which the universal Host upsent
> A shout that tore Hell's Concave, and beyond
> Frighted the Reign of *Chaos* and old Night.
> All in a moment through the gloom were seen
> Ten thousand Banners rise into the Air
> With Orient Colours waving: with them rose
> A Forest huge of Spears . . . (534-47).

As Allen comments: "The motion is hesitant and horizontal, but suddenly there is a quickening of movement and the vertical takes pre-eminence."[24] The symbolic aspect of this outward rise is ironically presented as the martial music of order,

---

[24] *Harmonious Vision,* p. 108. Like the minor crosscurrents in the light-dark pattern noticed just above, the "meteor" simile serves its traditional warning function even in the midst of so much brightness.

parody of heaven's marches (VI, 59-73), "rais'd / To highth of noblest temper Heroes old" (I, 552-3). Yet even as Satan surveys their "dazzling Arms," and all seems now a blaze of rising strength, building density through the comparisons with Greek and Arthurian warriors, the perspective is again suddenly if minutely adjusted to the reality of myth and place, as the catalogue of glory closes on another fall, "When *Charlemain* with all his Peerage fell / By *Fontarabbia*" (586-7).[25]

It is Satan, however, who is pre-eminent both in height and brightness above the massed rising of rebels, who "above the rest . . . Stood like a Towr," shining because:

> . . . his form had yet not lost
> All her Original brightness, nor appear'd
> Less then Arch Angel ruin'd, and th' excess
> Of Glory obscur'd: As when the Sun new ris'n
> Looks through the Horizontal misty Air
> Shorn of his Beams, or from behind the Moon
> In dim Eclipse disastrous twilight sheds (589-98).

The pattern of rising into light is now fully expressed, and yet there are the inevitable ironies. Satan's stature is self-reductive if we recall that, as we earlier found it on the lips of George Fox the Quaker, the "Tower" is a traditional epithet for Christ. And like the meteoric banner, the moon in eclipse is a portent, an image of darkness dimming the light (even as the strayed angels are only temporally arising so that they may eternally fall back into the palpable darkness of hell). And the sun is an image which spans both, with its traditional Christ analogy but yet with its rays dimmed like the moon, the symbol of energy debilitated and suggesting another leader of his people, shorn

---

[25] Cf. the comments by Broadbent, "Milton's Hell," p. 187.

Samson.[26] Nor is this quite all. "Dark'n'd so," continues Milton,
"yet shone"

> Above them all th' Arch Angel: but his face
> Deep scars of Thunder had intrencht . . . (599-601).[27]

The vertical movement again becomes absorbed into a joke
upon the fortunate fall, rhetorically stressed by the initial posi-
tioning of the key words; but in the course of the grim smile the
physical movement upward becomes illumination for the depths
of the spiritual abyss it plumbs even in rising. Satan himself
emphasizes this shift ironically when after describing the fall of
"Splendors" in a strife "not inglorious," he asserts that awareness of God's power could not have been reckoned "from the
Depth / Of knowledge past or present" (627-8). If one may
rephrase the metaphoric irony that is running through these
passages, it can be said that only abysmal ignorance could mis-
calculate so diabolically, could believe a God "upheld" by external forces had "wrought our fall" (638-42).

Then abruptly the slipping over into psychic levels is abandoned, and the hundred and fifty closing lines of the book
become literally spatial, beginning with the sense of vastnesses

---

[26] On this important description see Brooks, "Milton and the New Criticism," pp. 9-11 ("the simile is a microcosm of the whole poem"); MacCaffrey,
Paradise Lost as "Myth," pp. 173-4; Broadbent, "Milton's Hell," pp. 166-7.
To this latter source I owe the Samson analogy. Perhaps the best commentary is the most succinct: Svendsen, *Milton and Science,* pp. 69-70.

[27] It is customary to point out the parallels between heaven and hell, but
it may here be observed that parodic echoes occur within hell itself. When
Beelzebub later presents his crucial oration to the council, a speech "first
devis'd / By *Satan,* and in part propos'd" (II, 379-80), the description of
the speaker echoes that of Satan I have just quoted:

> . . . deep on his Front engraven
> Deliberation sat and public care;
> And Princely Counsel in his face yet shone,
> Majestic though in ruin . . . (II, 302-5).

beyond hell which will be the scene of the following books; this, too, in contrast with darkness:

> Space may produce new Worlds; . . .
>
> . . . and therein plant
> A generation, whom his choice regard
> Should favour . . .
> Thither, . . . shall be perhaps
> Our first eruption, thither or elsewhere:
> For this Infernal Pit shall never hold
> Celestial Spirits in Bondage, nor th' Abyss
> Long under darkness cover . . . (650-9).

Even so, we are not allowed to forget entirely the psychic level; at the end of this challenge and exhortation the millions of "flaming swords" are raised, "the sudden blaze / Far round illumin'd hell," and then all levels of literal and symbolic are confused as

> . . . highly they rag'd
> Against the Highest, and fierce with grasped Arms
> Clash'd on thir sounding shields the din of war,
> Hurling defiance toward the Vault of Heav'n (665-9).

But now all is light and gleam as heaven is introduced both in narrative retrospect and in parody into the antipodal confines of hell. Mammon leads the gold-mining expedition, and Pandemonium soon "Rose like an Exhalation" (710-1). Rajan has observed the irony that the gold which perverse Mammon delights in observing on the *floor* of heaven should be the climactic touch on the *roof* of Pandemonium; true light descends from God, false light rises from the depths.[28] And if this in-

---

[28] Rajan, *Paradise Lost and the Seventeenth Century Reader,* p. 47. Broadbent, "Milton's Hell," p. 180, comments that "Pandemonium rises as the

fernal temple is physically what Satan was in similitude, a
parody of "many a Tow'red structure high" (733), "in Heav'n
high Tow'rs," (749),[29] gleaming with "light / As from a sky"
(730) — if this is so, its golden aspiration, when "Th' ascending
pile / Stood fixt her stately highth" (722-3), must remind us not
only that her architect Mulciber fell, but that he fell with Satan
and those others made "Sufficient to have stood, though free to
fall." And the recollection leads us into the opening lines of
Book Two, where Satan seems to have become fused with his
own oriental palace and the precarious triumph of its gleaming
aspiration:

> High on a Throne of Royal State, which far
> Outshone the wealth of *Ormus* and of *Ind*,
> Or where the gorgeous East with richest hand

---

devils would like to rise; it provides artificial light and loftiness in the deep
dark pit of Hell." He emphasizes the pathos, perhaps underestimating the
impact of the sense that the fallen angels are, like Pandemonium, at this
moment in process of ascent. Mammon's inversions of the vertical-light scales
become crucial during his debate in council, when he theorizes that because
heaven "imitates" hell, hell can successfully imitate heaven — the theory,
indeed, not only for Pandemonium, but for all of the diabolic parodies of the
first two books is found in Mammon's argument:

> . . . How oft amidst
> Thick clouds and dark doth Heav'n's all-ruling Sire
> Choose to reside, his Glory unobscur'd,
> And with the Majesty of darkness round
> Covers his Throne; from whence deep thunders roar
> Must'ring thir rage, and Heav'n resembles Hell?
> As he our darkness, cannot we his Light
> Imitate as we please? This Desert soil
> Wants not her hidden lustre, Gems and Gold;
> Nor want we skill or art, from whence to raise
> Magnificence; and what can Heav'n show more? (II, 263-73).

The qualifying "unobscur'd" should have warned of a false analogy, of
course.
    [29] During the infernal debates both Moloch and Belial self-consciously use
"Heav'ns high Tow'rs" (II, 62, 129) as a synecdochic token of the dangerous
ascent being discussed.

Show'rs on her Kings *Barbaric* Pearl and Gold,
Satan exalted sat, by merit rais'd
To that bad eminence; and from despair
Thus high uplifted beyond hope, aspires
Beyond thus high, insatiate to pursue
Vain War with Heav'n . . . (II, 1-9).

Satan's first words provide a summary of both the structure and the significance of Book II. Here the archangelic leader makes explicit his ludicrous and terrible parody of the fortunate fall as it will be delineated by God's efforts:

. . . since no deep within her gulf can hold
Immortal vigor, though opprest and fall'n,
I give not Heav'n for lost. From this descent
Celestial virtues rising, will appear
More glorious and more dread than from no fall (II, 12-16).

Throughout the debate which follows, the physical pattern of the fall into darkness and the vainly hoped for resurrection into light obsess the psychology of all speakers. Moloch would "ascend" from the "dark opprobrious Den" to attack "Heav'n's high Tow'rs" (56-62), where is ensconced a "higher foe." Indeed, refusing the evidence of experience, he argues that "in our proper motion we ascend / Up to our native seat: descent and fall / To us is adverse" (75-7). "Th' ascent is easy then," he argues from "this abhorred deep" (81-7). But the specious argument on the physics of infernal motion is counterpointed by the narrator's borrowing of the vertical terms to describe the speaker: "he seem'd / For dignity compos'd and high exploit," but "his thoughts were low" (111, 115). Belial also plans action in a perspective of vertical motion, but he denies the inverted physics of Moloch, seeing that it is ultimately impossible that "all Hell should rise / With blackest Insurrection, to confound / Heav'n's purest Light" (135-7), that such an attempt could only produce a more horrible confusion and more "hideous fall / One day upon our heads" (177-8). Turning his oration, he jokes, rhetorically "so doubtful what might fall. / I laugh" (203-4) and advises patience in hell. But the last words reveal that he is, after all, as obsessed with impossibilities as Moloch. Such patience will eventually make "this darkness light" (220). It is, of course, Beelzebub who carries the day, and he sees the assault upon man as the fulfillment of Satan's promise of a fortunate fall: let us, he cries in closing, "our Joy upraise / In his disturbance; when his darling Sons / Hurl'd headlong to partake with us, shall curse / Thir frail Original" (372-5). We hear echoes of both the beginning and the close of the great pattern here perverted: from the beginning the description of the devils "Hurl'd headlong flaming", from the close, the description of Adam when the vision of Man's divine destiny has been given him and he stands "Replete with joy and wonder" (XII, 468).

So much for the planning; afterward, the entire movement of Book Two, and of those that follow, becomes an ascent into the light, almost from the moment in which Satan takes responsibility for closing the debate with his eulogy and promise: "Great things resolv'd, which from the lowest deep / Will once more lift us up" (392-3), "perhaps in view / Of those bright confines" (394-5), to

> Dwell not unvisited of Heav'n's fair Light
> Secure, and at the bright'ning Orient beam
> Purge off this gloom . . . (398-400).

This motif follows throughout as Satan moves with "deep thoughts" from "dark destruction," by his "resolution rais'd" toward the gates of hell and his encounter with Sin and Death.[30]

Yet there is a recurrent counterpoint which reiterates the metaphor of the spiritual abyss. "Whence / But from the Author of all ill could Spring / So *deep* a malice" (380-2), asks the narrator; and we find the devils pondering with "deep thoughts" (421), seized by "deep silence" (431), in "consultations dark" (486). And this undercurrent of descent in the ascendency comes into textural dominance through Sin's dreadful emphasis just as Satan is about to rise out of hell:

[30] The union of light and rising permeates the last half of Book II, of course, but see particularly lines 385-408, 434-40, 466, 468, 629-35, the pun in the simile at 642, the identification of Sin and Death with Night at 670, 714-20, 822-9, 864-94, 916. Even in the pattern of rising here, however, Milton enjoys monitory ironies. A notable example is the close of the meeting, when "they rose / Thir rising all at once was as the sound / Of Thunder heard remote" (475-7). The storm then enters a larger simile which reminds us that hell is its own place and will take its dark heart upward, even as it raised war in heaven from the spacious north, even as the devils first rose like a cloud of locusts off their infernal bed:

> Thus they thir doubtful consultations dark
> Ended rejoicing in their matchless Chief:
> As when from mountain tops the dusky clouds
> Ascending, while the North wind sleeps, o'erspread
> Heav'n's cheerful face, the low'ring Element
> Scowls o'er the dark'n'd lantskip Snow, or show'r (486-91).

It is, of course, an irony to be connected with the key description of Satan as a Sun "Shorn of his Beams": evil had dimmed the brightness of the burlesque God; now the darkened angels will burlesque God's power by enveloping the true Sun in their dusk. But the "joy" of Beelzebub's recent call to insidious assault echoes in the simile also, to promise the triumph of God, and this in the imagery of pastoral fitting to a commentary upon the projected field of struggle, Paradise:

> If chance the radiant Sun with farewell sweet
> Extend his ev'ning beam, the fields revive,
> The birds thir notes renew, and bleating herds
> Attest thir joy, that hill and valley rings. (492-5).

The "ev'ning beams" are not accidental either, for we shall find the evening hour a crucial symbolic setting for the bittersweet departure from Paradise, when infernal conquest brings on divine renewals.

> . . . down they fell
> Driv'n headlong from the Pitch of Heaven, down
> Into this Deep, and in the general fall
> I also . . . (771-4).

We are made suddenly to see again the first tableau of dazed
enervation when they were "Hurl'd headlong flaming . . . down,"
and to review the ironies which have led Satan to his paradoxical
resurgence. And we are better prepared for the most audacious
inversion of all, when Satan, promising "to set free / From out
this dark and dismal house of pain . . . all the heav'nly Host / Of
Spirits" (822-5), steps out of hell gate not into the light, but to
see:

> . . . in sudden view appear
> The secrets of the hoary deep, a dark
> Illimitable Ocean without bound,
>
> .   .   .   .
>
> . . . where eldest *Night*
> And *Chaos,* Ancestors of Nature, hold
> Eternal *Anarchy* . . . (890-6).[31]

It is a monitory moment in the pattern, as is Satan's first attempt
upon chaos, when the general upward movement is abruptly reversed and "all unawares / Flutt'ring his pennons vain plumb
down he drops / Ten thousand fadom deep" (932-4).

A monitory moment; but only that. Ascent is re-established,
and struggling upward through chaos Satan leads us at the
close of Book Two to a dawning view of the distant world of
light emerging above the borders of primordial darkness:

[31] On Chaos and old Night in relation to light, see Curry, *Milton's
Ontology,* pp. 84-6.

But now at last the sacred influence
Of light appears, and from the walls of Heav'n
Shoots far into the bosom of dim Night
A glimmering dawn; . . . (1034-7).

With Book Three we enter upon the poem's climactic vision of a world of light, pointed in three stages. The glimmering dawn at the close of Book Two is audaciously succeeded by the blazing intensity of the new invocation to "Holy Light," the "Bright effluence of bright essence increate." I shall argue more thoroughly later the role of Christ in the invocations; here it may suffice to recall that Hunter recently utilized important imagistic traditions to show that this light is the Son,[32] a proper aegis for a book which will reveal the heroic Redeemer whose love is the Light of the World, and whose first description within the poem is of one

Most glorious, in him all his Father shone
Substantially express'd, and in his face
Divine compassion visibly appear'd,
Love without end . . . (III, 139-42).

The second peak of intensity is the poem's highest moment on the scale of vertical ascent into light, the paradoxical vision of the Father and fountain, for like the Son, "God is light":

Fountain of Light, thyself invisible
Amidst the glorious brightness where thou sit'st
Thron'd inaccessible, but when thou shad'st
The full blaze of thy beams, and through a cloud

---

[32] "Holy Light in *'Paradise Lost.'*" Cf. the additional evidence in J. H. Adamson, "Milton's Arianism," *HTR*, LIII (1960), 269-76.

Drawn round about thee like a radiant Shrine,
Dark with excessive bright thy skirts appear,
Yet dazzle Heav'n, that brightest Seraphim
Approach not, but with both wings veil their eyes (III, 375-82).

When we reach this point, we realize that the scenic structure
of the epic has embraced the antipodes with a circling but steady
ascent from the bottomless abyss of darkness visible to the brightness invisible of the Almighty Father "High Thron'd above all
highth" (58).

But as God and Christ enact the ritual preparation for the
fortunate fall which will be the subject of the poem once it
enters the world of Man, we are made intensely conscious of
the vertical movement by a repetitive insistence upon sum-
marizing the journey in little. For instance, if God is seen "above
all highth," it is as he "bent *down* his eye" to watch the rising
flight of Satan, and from "high foreknowledge" to explain the
"high Decree" which leaves Man "free to fall" as those angels
"fell who fell."[33] And, of course, as he repeatedly invokes that
crucial word, as he watches the "present" and the "future"
hurtling headlong down upon Man, the vertical polarity is joined
in stress by luminosity. God and Christ's radiance, that of the
angels "thick as Stars" about them, is set against Satan's travels
"on this side Night / In the dun Air sublime" (71-2). It is the
air which envelops the fallen world, but the promise is made
to men that "I will clear thir senses dark" (188), so that "Light
after light well us'd they shall attain" (196). Christ's request to

---

[33] At one point the ambient refrain serves to give spatial dimension to
apparently abstract promise:

Upheld by me, yet once more he shall stand
On even ground against his mortal foe
By me upheld, that he may know how frail
His fall'n condition is. . . . (178-80).

die for Man takes up the insistent pattern of God's imagistic résumé: the anger will "fall" on him, death will place him "under his gloomy power," but he will not remain "inglorious," rather:

> I through the ample Air in Triumph high
> Shall lead Hell Captive maugre Hell, and show
> The powers of darkness bound. Thou at the sight
> Pleas'd, out of Heaven shalt look down and smile,
> While by thee rais'd I ruin all my Foes (254-8).

And at the Last Judgment Christ shall sit "Thron'd in highest bliss," prophesies the Father, "thy Humiliation shall exalt / with thee thy Manhood," while "they arraign'd shall sink / Beneath thy Sentence" (305-31).

As these verbal summaries recur we are made fully conscious of the manner in which the structure of vertical movements along a scale of luminosity has become symbolic of the "great argument." But it is perhaps only more slowly that the reader realizes that through the manipulation of scene, from the dark lake to the blinding throne, he has been led to mimetic enactment of precisely the promised resurrection into life which is the argument of the epic, an argument, moreover, never more explicit than just here at the close of the ascending action when it reaches the voice of God unfolding the plan of the *felix culpa*. We, not Adam, have climbed the *scala paradisa*.

This has been "argument," prophecy — the third stage of illumination comes in a return to narrative. Satan's journey is rejoined at the thin, bright edge of creation, where he finds "The luminous inferior Orbs, enclos'd / From *Chaos* and th' inroad of Darkness old" (420-1). The Satanic simile summarizes the symbolic narrative just enacted. Satan has like a "Scout / Through dark and desert ways with peril gone / All night" who

at the "cheerful dawn"[34] reaches "some high-climbing Hill" to
gasp at the sight of a metropolis:

> With glistering Spires and Pinnacles adorn'd,
> Which now the Rising Sun gilds with his beams (543-551).[35]

Then it happens. Satan sees the golden Sun itself, and drawn
as by the energy of its magnetic force drives toward this intensest
mode of physical light, "in splendor likest Heaven" (572).
Here "whence no way round / Shadow from body opaque can
fall," Satan "sharp'n'd his visual ray" (619-20) to descry Paradise. As readers, even at this third climactic light vision, we
have descended into a world of shadows, of dim imitations of
that divine blaze of God so recently viewed at the throne of
heaven. But for Satan the approach to the sun is an ascent, both
literally and in the resurgence of vital being he seeks from it.
And as we meet with him at "The place he found beyond expression bright," the converging movement of antagonist and
reader offers a poignant measure of the fall which has trapped
Satan within the confines of this little world of matter. Here
the lost leader can assume the guise of a "stripling Cherub"
with gold-spangled wings and gleaming wand. But when Uriel,
"the Angel bright . . . his radiant visage turnd" upon Satan
(645-6), we are abruptly conscious at his brightest moment that
the cherubic form is a poor mockery of past glory for he who
once was "of the first, / If not the first Arch-Angel" (V, 659-60).
He leaves the Sun, and:

[34] This recalls, of course, his first vision of light which "Shoots far into
the bosom of dim Night / A glimmering dawn" (II, 1036-7).
[35] Satan's journey, like God's interview, has been replete with dense awareness of the pattern of ascending and descending which gives to Book Three
a dizzying sense of multiplying repetitions; see III, 416-20, 485-90 (the
turbulences in the Limbo of Fools), 500-18, 523-5, 574.

> Down from th' Ecliptic, sped with hop'd success,
> Throws his steep flight in many an Aery wheel,
> Nor stay'd, till on *Niphates'* top he lights (740-2).

I take this last word of Book Three to be a pun ironically under-
lining the awareness that here he leaves behind all that is
angelic.[36] Now he will descend the chain of being as he adopts
a multitude of animal shapes until he ultimately lies writhing
in the ashes of his pride with all the hissing brood in living
emblem of his act. The ascent has been a paradox, the hard
search that hurtles pride more profoundly into itself:

> Which way I fly is Hell; myself am Hell;
> And in the lowest deep a lower deep
> Still threat'ning to devour me opens wide,
> To which the Hell I suffer seems a Heav'n (IV, 75-8).

But he has plunged not only into himself, but into temptation,
and so into time.

As Book Four opens, Milton associates Satan with "the Dragon"
of Revelations who "Came furious down," even as "*Satan,* now
first inflam'd with rage, came down" (IV, 3-9). The verb is
scriptural, but it inaugurates a subtle shift, an emphasis upon
willed swooping descent rather than retributive falling. It is
appropriate for that psychological moment in which Satan,
alone, looks into his own responsibility, exonerates God, and sees
the war within between self and self which made him both
active agent and sufferer when "Pride and worse Ambition
threw me down" (40). Like the narrative, the Satanic memory
will ascend for a moment to its former "bright eminence" to

---

[36] A pun reinforcing that at I, 226-8. Perhaps it is tactless to take as more
than coincidental the fact that "High" is the opening, "hies" the closing,
word of Book Two which narrates the ascent into creation.

admit that God supported him until he was self-abandoned to the abyss:

> . . . lifted up so high
> I sdein'd subjection, and thought one step higher
> Would set me highest . . . (49-51).

And ultimately, he accepts his inability to repent in terms of the symbolic function of scene in *his* imagination: "how soon / Would highth recall high thoughts" (95). And then he reverses the fortunate-fall paradox, bitter commentary upon his infernal adaptations of the theme:

> While they adore me on the Throne of Hell
> With Diadem and Sceptre high advanc'd
> The lower still I fall . . . (89-91).

As the narrative turns from diabolic meditation to Eden, the topography builds upward in lavish detail. Eden "crowns" a mountain, and about it "up grew / Insuperable highth of loftiest shade," "the ranks ascend / Shade above shade," "higher than thir tops" the wall "up sprung," "higher than that Wall" were other trees (135-46), the "Tree of Life, / High eminent" (218-9). Adam and Eve, first seen, image the aspiring pattern: "erect and tall / Godlike erect," in whom "thir glorious Maker shone" (288-9, 292). That there is tradition for it all should not discourage us from believing that these descriptions are assimilated into the symbolic pattern of the epic, from seeing them as physical types to remind one that if light emanates from the Father and fount, Raphael promises prelapsarian Adam that aspiration is not vain, because "Your bodies may at last turn all to Spirit. / Improv'd by tract of time, and wing'd ascend / Ethereal" (V, 497-9). But Satan has come to pervert this promise, to fell the "high advanc't / Creatures" from this "high seat" (359-60, 371).

With his coming there is another change in scenic texture, a definite turn and foreshadowing which thrusts us into the declining obscurity of Paradise lost.

Satan has come to Eden from the Sun "at highth of Noon" (564), but the emphasis in the earlier half of Book Four is dominantly vertical. Then Adam and Eve at the turn are exposed in a pun that resounds with the infernal snicker. It is simple: "to thir Supper Fruits they fell" (331). Immediately "the Sun / Declin'd" (352), evening comes, "and Twilight gray" (597).[37] Luminosity is the dominant scenic element, and it emerges strongly as symbol. If noon passes into evening, evening quickly gives way to night. But before it can do so, Milton reinforces the ominous joke, darkening the landscape by a tableau of fused light and darkness, descent and ascent, warning and promise that previews the final scene of the expulsion when Adam and Eve will look back upon lost Paradise to find the gate crowded with flaming guardians. It occurs when we are focused upon Gabriel, "Chief of th' Angelic Guards, awaiting night" (IV, 550) where:

> . . . the setting Sun
> Slowly descended, and with right aspect
> Against the eastern Gate of Paradise
> Levell'd his ev'ning Rays . . . (540-3).

When night succeeds to evening, it is the reflection of heaven, a time of rest and harmonies when one hears "Celestial voices to the midnight air" (682), a time when the stars "set and rise / Lest total darkness should by Night regain / Her old possession" (664-6). But in this gracious dimming of nature's eye there is already lowering that fall, whose signature rests with the dying

---

[37] Cf. IV, 352-5, 590-609, 792. Most telling, in view of Satan's usurpation of night in heaven as elsewhere, is Raphael's comment: "darkness there might well / Seem twilight here" (VI, 11-2); cf. also V, 642-6.

sun's rays upon the gate of Paradise. If there is a hymn to the
night, it is prelude to the pre-temptation of Eve in her dream.
The riptide of disturbance which the pieties of Adam direct
across the carefully established symbolic structure of darkness,
as well as across the natural sense of falling off from the brilliance
of Book Three, is soon turned back in irony by Satan. Surprised
by the guardians at Eve's ear, he ascends in "sudden blaze
diffus'd, inflames the Air" (818) and then emphasizing his
"high conceits," his "soaring" scorn and pride, his exchange
with the angels reminds him that all his "glory" now is the black
flame of passion, that he resembles now his "sin and place of
doom obscure and foul" (840). And the wedding of his symbolic darkness and the scenic dark of the narrative setting is
consummated — a point underlined in the last words of Book
Four — when Gabriel and his troop expel Satan from Paradise
and "with him fled the shades of night" (1015).

Book Five opens with the "Morn her rosy steps in th' Eastern
Clime / Advancing" (V, 1-2), as night and day begin to succeed
one another with regularity.[38] But it is day in a new Paradise,
one invaded by the spirit of Satan. And so, amid dazzling in-
sistences upon the "Morn return'd," the "day-spring," the "Sun
. . . up risen," falls the shadow of Eve's terrible dream of a night
walk with Satan. As she narrates her fears to Adam, she sets
the morning in a counterpoint of escape from the dark forces:
"glad I see / Thy face, and Morn return'd, for I this Night, /
Such night till this I never pass'd, have dream'd" (29-31).
Within the dream, the moon (already associated so closely with
Satan from the early similes) replaces the sun to throw all into
treacherous dimness: "Full Orb'd the Moon, and with more
pleasing light / Shadowy sets off the face of things" (42-3); and
in this obscure light (terrestrial image of darkness visible) the

---

[38] Which possibly is another reflection of Milton's debt to Spenser. In *The
Faerie Queene* one finds the most persistent pre-Miltonic development of a
poem which centers its light symbolism upon the recurrence of nightfall
and morning as a basic structural principle.

tree of knowledge seemed "Much fairer to my Fancy than by day" (53). And as this dream concludes, the darkness in light fuses into a vertical pattern, visible emblem in little of the fall:

> . . . Forthwith up to the Clouds
> With him I flew, . . .
>
> . . . .
> . . . wond'ring at my flight and change
> To this high exaltation; suddenly
> My Guide was gone, and I, methought, sunk down,
> And fell asleep . . . (86-92).

The dream is succeeded by Adam's assurances and the magnificent morning hymn with which poet and progenitor attempt to chase the shades of Satan's threat. But as the Sun, "who out of Darkness call'd up Light" (179), is invoked, the confusions within the creation of that light and darkness which have been so readily significant in heaven and hell begin to expound the theme anew. If before, we have ascended in imitation of the spiritual promise of man by traversing the abyss of dark to the towering throne of light, now all nature will image the kinship of fall and resurrection. "Thou Sun," prays Adam,

> of this great World both Eye and Soul,
> Acknowledge him thy Greater, sound his praise
> In thy eternal course, both when thou climb'st,
> And when high Noon hast gain'd, and when thou fall'st (171-4).

Joseph Summers has commented so admirably that one cannot do better than quote him: " 'Fall'st' occupies the strongest position as the final syllable of the line, the sentence . . . in the midst of praise we have approached the chief metaphysical theme of the poem, the Fall. It is true that the course of the sun

is regular and rhythmic and, under God's will, inevitable. But
the purpose, both theological and aesthetic, of the entire poem
is to show how the fall of man and Satan, although not inevitable, becomes within the light of all time and eternity a
part of the divine rhythm."[39] And we further observe that as
the hymn continues with "Mists and Exhalations that now rise,"
they are presented in descriptions of changing light, become
"falling showers," but "Rising or falling still advance his praise"
(185-92). The fortunate fall is God's praise, fortunate precisely
because it is a fall. But if God can subsume the alternations in
"goodness infinite," yet "God is Light," so that the hymn concludes in the unambiguous symbols of eternity:

> . . . if the night
> Have gathered aught of evil or conceal'd,
> Disperse it, as now light dispels the dark (206-8).

As if in response to the prayer, we find ourselves among the
"glittering Tents" with "Heav'n's high King" as he sends Raphael
to give Man warning of infernal dangers. Raphael is a darting
of light through light as "Veil'd with his gorgeous wings, up
springing light" (as so often with the word, a dual functioning
as substantive *and* verb), and "Flew through the midst of
Heav'n" (250-1). But his passage is downward, from the throne
through worlds to this world.[40] Satan has swooped down upon
the Garden in the figure of a cormorant, a black devourer "de-
vising Death / To them who liv'd" (IV, 196-7); Raphael's
descent serves as both contrast and parallel, he too coming as a

---

[39] " 'Grateful Vicissitude' in *Paradise Lost*," p. 259.
[40] M. M. Mahood, *Poetry and Humanism*, pp. 198-201, has a perceptive
analysis of the "motile" sense conveyed in this and other flights, tracing it
in part to Milton's interest in contemporary studies in the mechanics of
motion. In another place, this author suggests a conscious revolt against
Thomistic mechanics: see pp. 217, 321, n. 8.

bird, but as the fabled "Phoenix," who enshrines "his reliques in the Sun's / Bright Temple" (V, 272-4). The self-renewer, the sunbird, long assimilated to the Son in Christian iconography, is precisely appropriate for Raphael who comes as a proto-Christ continuing the polar opposition between the Son and Satan. For unlike the militant Michael, he teaches Adam "as friend with friend" (229), as a gentle instructor whose descent has been made only to herald a greater ascent, when men's

> . . . bodies may at last turn all to Spirit,
> Improv'd by tract of time, and wing'd ascend
> Ethereal . . . (497-9).

The angel and the message have come into a world bathed in the light of midday, reminder that Satan had come with the dark midnight. But his assurances end on a dreadful warning: ascent is for those who properly aspire, but "Some are fall'n, to disobedience fall'n, / And so from Heav'n to deepest Hell" (541-2). All is not well; Eve's dream has cast the dark shadow of the future across this book of the day; now Raphael's history of war in heaven will lengthen the shadows of the past; and when they meet, they will obscure the innocent glory of the present.

The innocence of Adam is nowhere more explicit than in this matter of light. In heaven he imagines "Sons of light, / . . . Day without Night, / Circle his Throne rejoicing" (160-3). In a new vision of glory we see just this, the "orders bright" before God's throne "when in Orbs / Of circuit inexpressible they stood, / Orb within Orb," "In song and dance about the sacred Hill" (594-5, 619). But Raphael carefully corrects Adam's misconception, explaining: "Time, though in Eternity, appli'd / To motion, measures all things durable / By present, past, and future" (580-2); assuring him: "wee have also our Ev'ning and our Morn, / Wee ours for change delectable, not need" (628-

9).[41] Heaven perhaps has not; but the poet has need of night in heaven. The brightest day in "Heav'n's great Year" is climaxed with a symbolic night, darkened — like that we have just passed through in Paradise — by Satan's evil:

> Deep malice thence conceiving and disdain,
> Soon as midnight brought on the dusky hour
> Friendliest to sleep and silence, he resolv'd
> With all his Legions to dislodge, and leave
> Unworshipt, unobey'd the Throne supreme (666-70).

The plotting takes place in an atmosphere of fevered haste, "ere yet dim Night / Her shadowy Cloud withdraws" (685-6), "now ere Night, / Now ere dim Night has disincumber'd Heav'n" (699-700). Milton marks the moment before Lucifer becomes Satan, before the irrevocable choice when he reviews the Satanic followers, "an Host / Innumerable as Stars of Night, / Or Stars of Morning" (745-6). Abdiel's debate with the falling will argue the relations between place and glory (811-2, 832-43), but the inversion of expectation which descries "Stars of Night" before "Stars of Morning" has already imaged the consequences of persuasion. The act of darkness done with Sin begins in a dark midnight in heaven, moves toward a midnight temptation in Eden, and ends in the eternal darkness visible of hell.

And it is perhaps time retrospectively to observe as schematic structure the pattern which has been developing. The first two books were enveloped in darkness, illuminated only by the struggle of the diabolic hosts to rise again toward the light. But if the following divisions of the poem narrated events enacted in the changing lights of nature, their emphasis can be clearly felt by recalling that Book Three opens with a plea for spiritual illumination from the "bright essence increate" followed by a

---

[41] Cf. V, 642-6, where Raphael cautiously describes heaven's "grateful Twilight (for Night comes not there in darker veil)."

narrative thrust into the blazing center of heaven; that Book Four opens with Satan's recriminations against the Sun (corresponding on the natural level to the life-giving Holy Light of Book III); that Book Five opens on morning's dawn in man's world; and that Book Six opens on morning in God's heaven. Light, as both cause and effect in heaven and upon earth, has been made the scenic center of these middle books of innocence between the fall of Satan and the fall of Man.

But to return to Book Six, we find Abdiel traveling through the night to emerge into that place-time where "Morn . . . Unbarr'd the gates of Light" (VI, 2-4), a journey which prompts the account of the cave within the Mount of God, where light and dark enact the vicissitudes of the whole poem, an interdependent exchange in which God utilizes dark as foil to the greater glory of the light: "Light issues forth, and at the other door / Obsequious darkness enters" (9-10). The adjective is able to call back the high pride of the Prince of Darkness, to comment upon his pretensions imagistically, as clearly as Abdiel will comment discursively in perceiving that "This is servitude, / To serve th' unwise, or him who hath rebell'd / Against his worthier" (178-81).

Then all is preparation as Abdiel is placed on a hill, "high applauded" and "more glorious" in return from among "so many Myriads fall'n" (24-43), a phrase which, like the reversed pattern of the angel-star image, warns that what has begun cannot be undone, for in eternity beginning is consummation. More often now we feel the interdependence of glory and evil, as the various descriptions of "grateful vicissitude" have made us feel the usefulness of darkness for the light. And so God in wrath darkens the mount, in "dusky wreaths, reluctant flames" (56-9) mirroring the scene we have viewed, the place God has now prepared, "His fiery *Chaos* to receive thir fall" (55). But Satan has begun his imitations of deity, "tow'ring," in "resemblance of the Highest,"

> High in the midst exalted as a God
> Th' Apostate in his Sun-bright Chariot sat
> Idol of Majesty Divine, enclos'd
> With Flaming Cherubim . . . (99-102).

If it echoes his earlier Sun epithets and the ironic heralding of his decline, the vignette is complicated in foreshadowing Christ's brilliant "Cherubic" "Chariot of Paternal Deity" (749-68), as well as the ultimate effect toward which the cosmic checking of Satan by Son and poet moves: the cherubim at "the Gate / With dreadful Faces throng'd and fiery Arms" (XII, 643-4). With the dawn, the narrative left Satan's rebels to join the rejoicing troops of God, using Abdiel's flight as the vehicle. The forces once joined in battle, we find the encounter described in the terms now so resonant of the argument: Gabriel "pierc'd the deep array / Of *Moloch*" (356-7), who was "Down clov'n to the waist" (361); and Michael's sword, "Descending . . . deep ent'ring," sheared Satan's side (325-6). But as battle proves indecisive, "Night her course began . . . over Heav'n / Inducing darkness" (406-7). With the night scene, one moves naturally to the diabolic camp; and it is in this night that Satan from "Deep under ground" digs "materials dark and crude" with which to prepare gunpowder, that curse of "dark Nativity" (470-82). Scene and symbol throughout, night at this point becomes an actor, willful abettor of evil: "So all ere day-spring, under conscious Night / Secret they finish'd" (521-2). With morning, the description again returns to the faithful angels; but as the rivals meet, heaven is darkened by the flame of the cannon, by the "Main Promontories flung" which "Came shadowing" until Satan's confused armies were "Under the weight of Mountains buried deep" with their engine (644-57). War lies underground, "fought in dismal shade" (666), the discomfiture an image of descent as mountains fall, as angels fall who in the beginning "Stood scoffing, highth'n'd in thir thoughts" (593, 628-9, 640 ff.). War, too, will image its own consequences in this physical narration of failure, of the proud preparations, the shining courage and challenge leading to the confused tumbling of pain-shocked warriors once "sufficient to have stood, though free to fall." They have chosen, and God chooses the Son on the third day to drive them "down / To chains of darkness" (738-9); hell is urging its shadow across heaven, even as heaven has been seen to create a continual, poignant counterpoint in hell.

As Christ emerges, he does so with his Father's glory, with the glistening chariot, and further continues the symbolic temporal round when he "rose / From the right hand of Glory where he sat, / And the third sacred Morn began to shine / Dawning through Heav'n" (746-9). If all is light in the scene, Christ is the terrible thunderer to the falling, who view his coming "Gloomy as Night" (832). His lightning loosed, the last lines echo with the terrible descent, repetition creating the sense of irreversible momentum: "down thir idle weapons dropp'd," "tempestuous fell / His arrows," he left them "spiritless, afflicted, fall'n" "Into the wasteful Deep," "headlong themselves they threw / Down . . . to the bottomless pit," "Nine days they fell" and felt "tenfold confusion in thir fall" — "deep fall / Of those too high aspiring" (838-900). The first half of the poem concludes, then, with the final telling of the first fall completed: "Hell saw / Heav'n ruining from Heav'n and would have fled / Affrighted; but strict Fate had cast too deep / Her dark foundations (867-70).

We have already heard the threat from God in heaven which at this halfway point Raphael voices for Adam: "firm they might have stood, Yet fell; remember, and fear to transgress" (911-12). Man too has been given the light of knowledge.

Prelude, then, has been made to the second fall, the fall of man. As Book Seven opens, the first word is "descend"; we are moving from the world of spirit into the world of nature, man's world. Having soared in the great "Empyreal Air" of heaven, the poet is half-regretful to return. But he fears that should he not, his pursuit of "Things unattempted yet in Prose or Rhyme" might breed just that dangerous pride he has so recently depicted as the beginning of evil, that he, too, might "from this flying Steed unrein'd . . . on th' *Aleian* Field . . . fall / Erroneous there to wander and forlorn" (VII, 17-20). Indeed, he finds himself a microcosmic mirror of his own argument, a later Adam

> . . . fall'n on evil days,
> On evil days though fall'n, and evil tongues;
> In darkness, and with dangers compast round (25-7).

The narrative, however, must begin at the beginning: the creation of this world now lapsed. Like the poet of the invocation, Raphael explains, Adam has shown no disobedience in questioning him concerning pneumatology, astronomy or genesis. But the very words of his reassurance carry for the reader the imagistic shadow of forbidden fruit and man's strange kinship with the serpent of darkness. Accept my discourse, warns Raphael, but,

> . . . beyond abstain
> To ask, nor let thine own inventions hope
> Things not reveal'd which th' invisible King,
> Only Omniscient hath suppret in Night (120-3).

God, darkener of his own brilliance before the angels, has his dark secrets from man as well. Fittingly; for that which he suppresses is that which Satan engenders, the knowledge not merely vain, which when seen will enter the paradoxical pattern of blindness by opening the eyes of the first parents and so darkening Paradise.

But the narrative setting for the interview is still midday

(98-101) because the narrative within the narrative, Raphael's history, is to tell of the bringing of light out of darkness. "Let there be Light, said God" (243); so begins the creation, and the entire account is bathed in this energy of glory, energy transferred to the sun, "great Palace now of Light" (354-63), energy diffused through "thousand lesser Lights dividual" which were as "bright Luminaries that Set and Rose" (375-85). All is light, and its coming into being has the familiar accompaniment of ascent. Christ was "uplifted" on cherubic wings as he purged "downward" the "black tartareous cold Infernal dregs" of the abyss so that light might "spring" from the deep (220-46); hills appear "high as heav'd" (288), swans "rising on stiff Pennons, tow'r" (441), the beasts "in broad Herds upsprung," "as the Mole / Rising" or "bleating rose / As Plants" (458-80). Having drawn forth this world, culminating in the creation of Man, ("erect / His Stature, and upright"), the Son "up return'd / Up to the Heav'n of Heav'ns his high abode," and with him "the bright Pomp ascended jubilant" (551-85). But the most notable aspect of the vertical movement is the development of an elaborate contrast between Satan's fall and man's ascent as well as Christ's. Raphael begins the entire account of creation with a summary of the argument of the immediately preceding books:

> Know then, that after *Lucifer* from Heav'n
> (So call him, brighter once amidst the Host
> Of Angels, than that Star the Stars among)
> Fell with his flaming Legions through the Deep
> Into his place, and the great Son return'd
> Victorious with his Saints . . . (131-6).

This serves to initiate a description of how Man was created to frustrate the spirit of Satan, "lest his heart exalt him in the harm / Already done" (150-1), in spite of his failure to win "this high Temple," to topple "This inaccessible high strength"

(148, 141). The plan is unfolded once more in vertical terms: Man and his world can dwell together,

> . . . till by degrees of merit rais'd
> They open to themselves at length the way
> Up hither, under long obedience tri'd (157-9).

The first question is why Satan should appear at all in this juncture of the narrative; the second why he should appear so explicitly as Lucifer the light-bringer, just at that moment when we are receiving the account of Christ drawing forth light out of the deep. The answer to both questions lies in the complex relation between good and evil which has been developing imagistically ever since the great affirmation of the morning hymn which revealed God's potency so starkly in those vertical terms most crucial to the argument: "Rising or falling still advance his praise." In that hymn, too, it will be recalled, Adam addressed Lucifer-Venus, ambiguous glory,

> Fairest of Stars, last in the train of Night,
> If better thou belong not to the dawn,
> Sure pledge of day, that crown'st the smiling Morn (V, 166-8).

This ambiguity in nature was reflected metaphorically, as we saw, at the moment of turning in heaven, when the rebel host were yet indeterminate, "Stars of Night, / Or Stars of Morning" (745-6). Empson observed the difficulties of Milton's stellar imagery, commenting on Christ's role in *Paradise Regained* as the Morning Star, "who is Lucifer, who is Satan," and observing that in Adam's hymn his star "may belong to Christ or Satan."[42]

---

[42] William Empson, *Some Versions of Pastoral*, pp. 181-5. Empson does not observe that there is scriptural precedent for both Lucifer (Isaiah 14:12) and Christ (Revelations 2:28, 22:16) as Morning Star. Such precedents, however, must be absorbed into the internal order of a poet's symbolic structure; I merely wish to avoid any implication that Milton was creating a daring innovation, or exposing a latent Manichaean psychology.

Certainly he is right in emphasizing a Christ-Satan relationship, but there is more to be said of the matter than his rather misleading discovery of "a secret parallel between the two."

It is salutary to recall the caveat issued by Rosemond Tuve in connection with her own reading of *Comus:* "One is only warned not to put 'good' or 'bad' beside any object and then follow some 'pattern of symbols,' but rather to watch the symbols infallibly develop before us complexities we had not suspected, in a pattern which they do not provide, but follow."[43] It will scarcely be necessary at this point to remind the reader that neither Miss Tuve nor I imply any simplistic ornamental theory in so asserting; we could certainly agree that the "argument" cannot be discursively sustained or paraphrased, but exists through an act of imagistic mimesis. But it has been my effort in an earlier chapter to demonstrate also that the images are dominated by *topoi* whose discursive futility arises from their own metaphoric origins. Here, of course, is a hint of their nature. The perennial tropes of Christianity, of religion itself, are metaphors precisely because they reflect modes of thinking which defy the normal processes of linear syntax, because they are paradoxes. And it should be clear by this stage in our discussion of *Paradise Lost* that the pattern which the images "follow" is no idea, not even the central one of the fortunate fall, but a mode of experiencing which infects the affective purity of every image; put simply, the mode of paradox.[44]

The paradox is complex, involving the interlocking efforts of contrary wills. It is too easy to remember the triumphant paean

---

[43] *Images and Themes in Five Poems by Milton,* p. 153.

[44] For a traditional reaction against claims for the importance of paradox in evaluating Milton, see Rajan, *Paradise Lost and the Seventeenth Century Reader,* pp. 124-5; the view persists in Colie, "Time and Eternity," *JWCI,* XXIII (1960), 127. For a sympathetic view see Svendsen, *Milton and Science,* pp. 232-5, an important analysis of Milton's way with symbols. Arthur Barker, "Structural Pattern in *Paradise Lost*," *PQ,* XXVIII (1949), 29-30, demonstrates how even the order of books "serves chiefly to sustain the Christian paradox" by setting tragic against Virgilian patterns.

of Adam to that goodness infinite who "all this good of evil
shall produce" at the close, so that we may forget Satan's fuller
version at the beginning:

> . . . If then his Providence
> Out of our evil seek to bring forth good,
> Our labour must be to pervert that end,
> And out of good still to find means of evil (I, 162-5).

God is victor, but he is victor upon terms of Satan's instrumentality. Man's resurrection will coincide with Satan's final
fall, but only after Satan's rising has occasioned man's fall. It is
disconcerting to realize that "Rising or falling still advance his
praise" might be said of Satan, as of God, with profoundest
meaning. The difficulty here, however, is less in conceiving the
paradox than in disentangling its terms from conceptualization
long enough to feel on the pulses how shockingly tense their
coexistence makes any comfortably orthodox relationship with
evil.

It is less easy, however, to absorb light and darkness into a
satisfactory *concordia discors* because they are substantive rather
then relational in normal discourse. Therefore, it may be best
to turn from light symbols to review the germane area of sight,
from substantive to act, before attempting a further look at the
Lucifer problem. If light is a value symbol, sight reflexively becomes a positive quality. But we have found that Satan persuades
Eve that natural sight (from the opening of the poem it is fused
with insight) is inadequate ("your Eyes that seem so clear, / Yet
are but dim"), and that man and Milton pervert seeing into a
symbol of primal disobedience ("thir Eyes how op'nd, and thir
minds / How dark'nd"). Looking where they should not for
knowledge ("Things not reveal'd which th' . . . Omniscient
hath supprest in Night"), they are blinded. Sight, then, as
symbol, has been distorted from its regular associative channels

and become evil. But God, like the blind poet, can take nature's evil and convert it to spiritual good. Therefore, in gracing Adam with the vision of comfort, he converts perversion, purges the natural eye into physical blindness (accepting the inversion of values enforced by Satan) that it may see "things invisible to mortal sight." Now, it is perfectly clear that there are limits beyond which liberty in manipulating traditional symbols becomes license. And it is equally clear that in a poem which repeatedly depicts God, the sun and the vigilant angels through the synecdoche of the "eye"[45] such liberty is unlikely to be taken with sight imagery. I review here this particular nexus of related passages in order to suggest that Milton does manipulate his metaphors dynamically, and that he is saved from either a too straitened traditionalism or a personal arbitrariness by allowing the mode of paradox to govern his associations. For if paradox raises novelties, it falls back upon normal expectations to illuminate them; it is a rebel bound to orthodoxy. Within such an organization, the limits are polarities; anchored in the solidity of the great paradoxes, each local image is free to reveal itself or to deny itself by completing the embrace of its inverted alter ego, as Eros completes his being in Anteros, as the Renaissance finds Diana in Venus.[46]

What are we to say, then, of the full complexity of the Lucifer passage in Book Seven? To see the bright star dropping into darkness sharpens the contrast implicit in every instance of vertical movement through a scale of luminosity when that picture is set in such close juxtaposition to Christ's depression of darkness whence

[45] III, 58-9, 576 ff., 650, 660; IV, 300; V, 171, 711-8.
[46] My description is applicable to the functioning of paradox. But it is worth while to remark that my mythic metaphors are borrowed from active Renaissance traditions of *discordia concors*. The discussions in Edgar Wind, *Pagan Mysteries of the Renaissance* (New Haven, 1958), reveal how deeply paradox invaded the iconography of the era, with particular emphasis upon the Ficino circle and Spenser, two important traditions in Milton's background.

> . . . Light
> Ethereal, first of things, quintessence pure
> Sprung from the Deep, and from her Native East
> To journey through the airy gloom began (243-6).

The juxtaposition does more, however. It reminds us of the hidden terror inevitable in the paradox of the fortunate fall, that aspect which has led some critics to deny that Milton embraced the conception. For if we find light rising out of darkness, we also perceive here the clearly-etched obverse: the origin of visible darkness in the fall of the illuminated from light. Nowhere in the poem are threat and hope more inseparably twinned. Nor can the intercalation of Satan as Lucifer at this point fail as ironic commentary upon the diabolic debate and soliloquy we have heard. His stellar brightness being averred by the angel voice itself, the analogy reminds us that the Son is in the act of creating the stars, that the Luciferian brightness is to the Son's as that of the brightest star to the sun's:

> Hither as to thir Fountain other Stars
> Repairing, in thir gold'n Urns draw Light,
> And hence the Morning Planet gilds her horns (364-6).

The point will be reinforced once more, when Satan is for the second time nominated "*Lucifer*, so by allusion call'd, / Of that bright Star to *Satan* paragon'd" (X, 425-6). This is at the moment of his descent into hell to boast of the corruption of man, the moment in which he "Star-bright appear'd, or brighter" (450), but clad merely, like his star, in "permissive glory" (451). And here his part in the history of the paradoxical fall pattern will be finally closed, as brightness, eminence, and triumph sink under God's emblematic justice.

The pattern is completed only in the closing lines of the epic, when Christ assumes the star associations of which the serpentine

Satan has been shorn, but this time with the ambiguities of the morning-evening star resolved, with light risen and darkness buried:

> . . . so he dies,
> But soon revives, Death over him no power
> Shall long usurp; ere the third dawning light
> Return, the Stars of Morn shall see him rise
> Out of his grave, fresh as the dawning light,
> Thy ransom paid, which Man from death redeems,
> .   .   .   .
> . . . this act
> Shall bruise the head of *Satan,* crush his strength
> Defeating Sin and Death, his two main arms,
> And fix far deeper in his head thir stings (XII, 419-32).[47]

It is this voice of hope which Adam answers when he cries out of his vision of the fortunate fall:

> O goodness infinite, goodness immense!
> That all this good of evil shall produce,
> And evil turn to good; more wonderful
> Than that which by creation first brought forth
> Light out of darkness! (469-73).

In Milton's paradoxical symbolic, light carries the potentiality of darkness, as sight carries the potentiality of blindness. The archangel as Lucifer is the imagistic assurance that he was created "sufficient to have stood"; his Satanic darkness that he was also created "free to fall." Passing briefly over Book Eight, let us apply this lesson to the crucial scene of man's fall.

---

[47] Cf. "at his Birth a Star / Unseen before in Heav'n proclaims him come" (XII, 360-1).

At the close of Book Seven, "Ev'ning arose in *Eden*, for the Sun / Was set, and twilight from the East came on" (582-3), and the emphasis upon the time of day continues on into the following books.[48] In the Eighth Book, as Adam recounts his own history in return for Raphael's instruction, this universal evening of the creation fuses with the evening of another day in Paradise, until Raphael, while "the parting Sun / Beyond the Earth's green Cape and verdant Isles / *Hesperian* sets" (630-2), repeats once more the formula of the fall: "stand fast; to stand or fall / Free in thine own Arbitrement it lies" (640-1). "So saying he arose" (644). The idyl is ended, and at his rising, the angel's warning prepares the way for the catastrophe which will strike in Book Nine. And, properly, the book which changes the poet's "Notes to Tragic" opens in the deepening shade of Satan: "By Night he fled, and at Midnight return'd" (IX, 58). We learn how, "cautious of day" since his disguise had been penetrated by Uriel,

> The space of seven continu'd Nights he rode
> With darkness, thrice the Equinoctial Line
> He circl'd, four times cross'd the Car of Night
> From Pole to Pole . . . (63-6).

and when he returns, "with inspection deep" (83) he considers until he finds the serpent fittest "To enter, and his dark suggestions hide" (90). Envying the circling stars that "bear thir bright officious Lamps, / Light above Light" (104-5), he boasts

---

[48] The only other light passage of great interest in Book Eight is that in which Adam explains that when he learned he could name whatever he saw, he first turned to the great luminary: "Thou Sun, said I, fair Light, / And thou enlight'n'd Earth" (VIII, 273-4). The refrain of ascent and light, of course continues throughout the Book as an undercurrent: see lines 87-8, 90-1, 97, 121, 126, 150-1, 155-6, 157, 160-4, 172, 178, 198-200, 245, 296, 303, 315-6, 350-1, 358, 367-8, 410, 413, 430, 432, 454-9, 464, 521, 551, 586, 592-3, 598, 617-8, 643, 653.

how in "one Night" he and his own will be freed from "servitude inglorious" (140-1); then, "wrapt in mist / Of midnight vapour," he seeks out the serpent which will "hide me, and the dark intent I bring" (158-62). "Like a black mist low creeping, he held on / His midnight search" (180-1) — a passage climaxing this indeterminate literalness with the diabolic axiom that "who aspires must down as low / As high he soar'd" (169-70).

But morning follows this threateningly metaphoric night, and Eve falls, a matter repeatedly insisted upon, at high noon (IX, 219, 397-403, 739-44). This nonscriptural particular has not greatly exercised Miltonic expositors: Kelley attributes it to Milton's desire to found the sin of gluttony in the fall through reference to the hour that "wak'd / An eager appetite," and McColley suggests that it results from traditional plans of analogy between the fall and crucifixion.[49] Both rationales are only locally suitable, implying unconcern with the internal values which have accrued to the sun, and it would seem more cautious to accept these theological resonances as gratuitous overtones given off by a more decorous symbol.

First, for some tradition which encouraged Milton to build the noonday into his light symbolism. The Old Testament contains four passages in which the noon figures as a symbol for man's disregard of God's aid. Deuteronomy 28:28-29 warns that for disobedience "The Lord shall smite thee with madness and blindness. . . . And thou shalt grope at noonday, as the blind gropeth in darkness." Job 5:14 teaches that the "crafty" and the "froward" "meete with darkness in the daytime, and grope in the noonday as in the night." Isaiah 59:10 says that through sin "we grope for the wall like the blind, and we grope as if we had no eyes: we stumble at noonday as in the night." These passages, of course, echo the ironic comments at Genesis 3:5-7 on the opening of Adam and Eve's eyes at the fall — comments

[49] Kelley, *This Great Argument,* p. 148; Grant McColley, *Paradise Lost: An Account of its Growth and Major Origins* (Chicago, 1940), pp. 160-1.

worked by Milton into his elaborate construction of complex
sight-in-blindness paradoxes. This being true, perhaps it is
natural enough for him to associate the temptation with noon.
But the more likely primary cause is a description in Psalm
91:6 of "the destruction that wasteth at noonday." So reads the
King James translation; but in the Vulgate the verse more
strikingly speaks of a "daemonio meridiano" who appears Eng-
lished in the Douai-Rheims version as "the midday divel."[50]

Jeremy Taylor referred to this text in a Whitsunday sermon
against spiritual unwariness in those who (like the Eve who
forgets her diabolic nightmare to rush quickly into the devil's
orchard) "suppose that unclean spirits walk in the night":

> so it used to be; 'for they that are drunk are drunk in the night,'
> said the apostle. But Suidas tells of certain *empusae* that used to
> appear at noon, at such times as the Greeks did celebrate the
> funerals of the dead; and at this day some of the Russians fear
> the noon-day devil. . . . The prophet David speaketh of both
> kinds, 'Thou shalt not be afraid for the terror by night; and *a
> ruina et daemonio meridiano*, 'from the devil at noon thou shalt
> be free.' It were happy if we were so; but besides the solemn
> followers of the works of darkness in the times and proper

[50] I cite from *Biblia Sacra Veteris et Novi Testamenti* . . . apud Petrum
Santandreanum (n.p., 1574) and the Douai: *The Holie Bible. By the English College of Doway* (Douai, 1609-10). In both instances, of course, the
Psalm is numbered "ninety." Among the reformers' translations, only one
carried the literal reference into English. Wycliffe translated: "fro the
inrennyng, and the middai deuel" (*The Holy Bible . . . made from the Latin
Vulgate by John Wycliffe and his Followers*, ed. J. Forshall and F. Madden
[Oxford, 1850]). The Bishops' Bible had spoken of "any deadly fyt that
destroyeth at hygh noone" (*The holie Bible* [colophon:] Imprinted at London in powles Churchyarde [1568]), and the Geneva and Breeches Bibles
(one or both of which Milton owned: see Wynne E. Baxter, "Milton's
Bibles," *N&Q*, ser. II, vol. III [1911], 109-11) agreed on "the plague that
destroyeth at noone day" (*The Bible and Holy Scriptures translated according to the Ebrue and Greke* [Geneva, 1569], and *The Bible, that is the Holy
Scripture* [Imprinted at London by Robert Barker, 1610]).

seasons of darkness, there are very many who act their scenes of darkness in the face of the sun, in open defiance of God. . . .[51]

Augustine would have agreed that this was the major lesson of the passage: "*Non timebis a timore nocturno, a sagitta volante per diem, a negotio perambulante in tenebris, a ruina et daemonio meridiano*. . . . Quid est timendum in nocte, et quid in die? Cum quisque ignorans peccat, tanquam in nocte peccat: cum autem sciens peccat, tanquam in die peccat." And further, he would associate the passage explicitly with temptation: "Tentationem quae fit in ignorantibus levis, timorem nocturnum appellavit; et tentationem quae fit in scientibus levis, sagittam volantem per diem appellavit."[52] If this strand of tradition is relevant to Eve, the tempted, Augustine's critic St. Jerome popularized a gloss which emphasized the tempter: "the devil, in the disguise of an angel of light, has his ministers disguised as ministers of justice (2. Cor. 11.14f.). . . . [We] shall understand by noonday demons the heresiarchs who, in the disguise of angels of light, preach the doctrine of darkness."[53] In this and the many like readings of the Psalm which followed upon it, we can recognize not only the justification for Satan's appeal to Eve's sense of desert, but for his earlier arrival as a false angel upon the sun where all was "Sun-

---

[51] Jeremy Taylor, *The Whole Works* ed. R. Heber and rev. C. P. Eden (London, 1883), IV, 350. Taylor's reference is to *Suidae historica* (Basil, 1564), col. 294: "Empusa, seu Onocole: spectrum diabolicum, ab Hecate immissum, & calamitosis apparens, quod in uarias figuras se transformare putatur. inde dictum, quod uno pede incedat, alterum uero habeat aeneum aut asininum. Putabatur autem etiam in meridie apparere, cum defunctis inferiae ferrentur. Aristophanes in Ranis: at medius fidius belluam uideo magnam. Cuiusmodi? terribilem, multiformem. Iam enim bos fit, iam mulus, alias formosissima foemina. Vbi est? accedam ad eam. At foemina esse desiit, iam canis est. Empusa igitur est. Igne certe quidem tota collucet facies, & pedem habet aeneum."

[52] *Enarrationes in psalmos* xc. 7; PL XXXVII, 1153-4. The Vulgate differs in small particulars, notably in substituting "incursu" for Augustine's "ruina."

[53] Augustinian and Hieronymaic traditions are both thoroughly outlined in Rudolph Arbesmann, "The 'Daemonium Meridianum' and Greek and Latin Patristic Exegesis," *Traditio*, XIV (1958), 17-31, a valuable essay brought to my attention by Mr. Edward Foye; I cite from p. 26.

shine, as when his Beams at Noon Culminate from th' *Equator*"
(III, 616-7).

I think it worth while to observe that the notable scriptural
epic from which, I am convinced, Milton both borrowed and
learned a great deal, Joseph Beaumont's *Psyche,* is the only other
Renaissance poem on the fall which makes emphatic reference
to the temptation occurring at noon.[54] Satan there finds the serpent, "whose illustrious skin / Play'd with the Sun . . . all heav'n's
highnoon face" (VI, 256). Like Milton, Beaumont elaborates a
multitude of variations upon the ironic vision given by the fruit,
"a bright Morn of Science" from the "enlightning *Tree*" which
cleared for the serpent the "Mists of Ignorance whose thick disguise . . . kept me down a beast / As dark and dull as any of the
rest" (VI, 283-5). But for our purpose, the interest lies in *Psyche*
carrying a repetitive current of references to the noonday sun
which make it quite obvious that, although the long mythic
poem has none of Milton's overall symbolic consistency, yet the
hour of Beaumont's temptation scene is implicated in a pattern
signally close in import to what Taylor and Augustine em-
broidered around the Psalm. Perhaps the best instance is provided by Beaumont's description of Christ's face at the nativity,

> . . . by whose soul-piercing raies
> The *Gentiles,* quite dam'd up til now in night,
> Admonish'd are to understand their waies
> And tread the open paths of highnoon Light (VIII, 36).

When this offered grace is refused, occasioning the flight into
Egypt, God looses Vengeance, whose

[54] My own conviction of Beaumont's significance to Milton is in part borne
out by the researches of Alexander B. Grosart in the "Memorial-Introduc-
tion" to his edition of *Complete Poems of Dr. Joseph Beaumont* (Edinburgh,
1880), I, xlvii, lix-lxi, and Grant McColley, *Paradise Lost,* pp. 33, 51, 80,
85, 98-101, 122, 125, 134-7, 144, 172-82, 203, 252, 323. All references are to
the Grosart edition.

. . . eyes were constant Lightning, flashing down
Her fiery Cheeks, and with their sprightful motion
Glancing a more than highnoon Day upon
The frighted Night of that black Region (VIII, 111).

Milton himself had utilized this ambivalence in the Elder
Brother's capstone to the *consolatio* in *Comus:*

He that has light within his own clear breast
May sit i' th' centre, and enjoy bright day,
But he that hides a dark soul and foul thoughts
Benighted walks under the mid-day Sun;
Himself is his own dungeon (381-5).[55]

It seems to me improbable in a high degree that the poet who
from fifteen years of age into his maturity composed metrical
paraphrases of the Psalms would have written such lines without recalling the "daemonio meridiano" passage, or that he
would have given such attention to the Psalms without becoming
aware of the exegetical traditions. Even so, tradition could only
offer Milton materials; it was his obligation to utilize those materials in coherence with his entire symbolic construct. I have
paused so long in preparation because the high noon of the
temptation seems to me a signal point in the epic for which
Milton prepares with exceptional care.

The noonday appears early, in one of the most frequently-
admired purple passages, the fall of Mulciber:

. . . from Morn
To Noon he fell, from Noon to dewy Eve,
A Summer's day; and with the setting Sun
Fell from the Zenith like a falling Star (I, 743-5).

[55] Cf. Tuve, *Images and Themes,* pp. 150-1, whose reading is borne out by
the tradition I have cited.

It has been argued that this description interjects a note of assurance of calm in the midst of infernal confusion; quite the
opposite is true.[56] In Mulciber's fall we have the first echo of
the interwoven spatial-temporal terms of "Nine times the Space
that measures Day and Night." But this is a richer instance,
the word "noon" itself having a spatial dimension as well as a
temporal in the Renaissance, frequently indicating the culminating position in a movement, literal or conceptual. When
we read how the archangelic architect fell "from Morn / To
Noon," this aspect of the word enhances the spatial sense, only
to immediately pose a paradox — one we have been learning
conceptually and imagistically throughout the opening book:
that one rises to fall (this half supplied by the Vulcanian myth
in which Mulciber is embedded) and falls to rise (this half,
by the spatial sense of the word itself).

However, another problem immediately must be raised. If
the First Book has been unambiguous in equating ascent with
light, descent with darkness, how does one fall from "morn"
into the peak intensity of light at noon? Like the other, this
problem dissolves in the history of the word, which quite com-
monly indicated its Satanic obverse, midnight, as well as midday
itself during the Renaissance.[57] Milton was gifted by history
with a single word, then, whose paradoxical significations embraced in epitome both extremities of his light symbolism as well
as a third dimension of space which superimposed this natural
paradox upon his other pattern of symbolic spatial movement.
Nor was it anything but fortunate for a Christian epic that this
inherent darkness at noon had its origins in the circumstances
of the crucifixion. I would see, then, the whole pattern of Milton's symbolism overlaid upon the apparent idyllic naturalism

[56] Geoffrey Hartman, "Milton's Counterplot," *ELH,* XXV (1958), 1-12,
esp. 2-3.
[57] I am indebted to the OED for my history; Milton's line is one of
numerous illustrations of this latter usage: "the wandring Moon / Riding
near her highest noon" ("Il Penseroso," line 68).

of the genre miniature of a classical Mulciber. And in the following lines I would see the falling, dimming star of the Lucifer tradition uniting with the evening sun of that long day's dying in the last books. Finally, finding "noon" here used for the first time as the measure for a fall, I would see an ambiguous promise of a later fall and its victim in that description of how the demon fell "from Noon to dewy Eve."

The ominous quiet of the midsummer day through which Mulciber falls is soon caught up in a simile for the silent attention of the infernal host before Beelzebub's critically influential speech, when they stood "still as Night / Or Summer's Noon-tide air" (II, 308-9); here the paradoxical darkness-in-light implications of the word are separated for explicit acknowledgment. The sun offers no obstacle to sight, "nor shade, / But all Sun-shine, as when his Beams at Noon / Culminate" (III, 615-7), and Satan's first betrayal of Uriel upon that flaming orb takes place "at highth of Noon" (IV, 564). The hypocrisy which "neither Man nor Angel can discern" is unrevealed even in light upon light. We have above examined the third point of intensity in the series of "high Noon" preparations for the fall of Man, the culminating line of Adam's sun-hymn which unites light and darkness, climbing and falling as intricately as the Mulciber description.

Now let us reconsider the fall at noon. It comes, as does the betrayal of Uriel, from the Prince of Darkness garbed in glittering hypocrisy, even standing in that posture so often attributed to Man throughout the poem for all that it implies: "erect." He on "rising folds" "tow'r'd," "Carbuncle his Eyes; / With burnisht Neck of verdant Gold, erect" (IX, 498-501). His midnight mists are cast off before Eve, but his associations with the paradoxical "noon" and all that has been built about it, make him for the reader the literal embodiment of the *daemonio meridiano*, reminding us in another framework of his ambiguous Lucifer phase.

As Eve reaches toward death under the noonday sun, we hear the echoes of Augustine, "cum autem sciens peccat, tanquam in die peccat," or of Taylor, "there are very many who act their scenes of darkness in the face of the sun, in open defiance of God." And we are also authorized to hear the echo of Milton the young pamphleteer warning his fellow Puritans against letting lapse the clear grace of God's favor offered them through the successes of the early Reformation: "O if we freeze at noone after their earley thaw, let us feare lest the Sunne for ever hide himselfe, and turn his orient steps from our ungrateful horizon justly condemned to be eternally benighted."[58]

The weakening of Eve has come in the dream; her temptation has come in the invisible robes of hypocrisy; but the choice (for reason also is choice) has been from Eve's consciousness: "in her ears the sound / Yet rung of his persuasive words, impregn'd / With Reason, to her seeming, and with Truth" (IX, 736-8). The high noon setting is a static symbol for that long hortatory history of Satan with which Raphael enlightened the mind of man in the books that went before. But the candle of the Lord has flickered out.

We have earlier seen how this ironically brilliant fall flows into that other irony of the first parents' eyes being opened to blindness, of their falling where they expect to soar. These effects are revealed in the first guilty sexual union, and the expression of sexuality through floral images which we have also noted should prepare us for one of the most poignant versions of vertical descent which threads through this Ninth Book, one which unites Man and nature in the consequences of sin. Satan first finds Eve alone while she is tending:

[58] *Animadversions,* in *Yale Prose Works,* I, 705. The pattern is adumbrated again in *Samson Agonistes,* where the chorus warns that God often strikes down his great agents "Amidst thir highth of noon" (683), with obvious reference to Samson's blindness, a blindness which let him see inwardly as does the poet, as does Adam, and so avenge God upon the Philistines when "The Feast and noon grew high" (1612).

Each Flow'r of slender stalk, whose head . . .

. . . .

Hung drooping unsustain'd, them she upstays
Gently with Myrtle band, mindless the while,
Herself, though fairest unsupported Flow'r (IX, 428-33).

After she has eaten, "hight'n'd as with Wine" through "expectation high / Of knowledge" (788-93), Eve comes to Adam who immediately recognizes some terrible change, and unawares, perpetrates the loveliest symbolic act of all the poem:

From his slack hand the Garland wreath'd for *Eve*
Down dropp'd and all the faded Roses shed (892-3).[59]

It has all come about through the rise of Satan from hell into Paradise: all nature ruined, and man; which makes it appropriate again that false notes rising in the microcosm should, like the tempter, come from below:

. . . high Winds worse within
Began to rise, high Passions, Anger, Hate,
Mistrust, Suspicion, Discord, . . .

. . . .

. . . sensual Appetite, who from beneath
Usurping over sovran Reason claim'd
Superior sway . . . (1122-31).

---

[59] This falling floral imagery recurs once more when Eve learns that they must leave the Garden, and cries out as her first reaction, "O flow'rs,"

. . . which I bred up with tender hand
From the first op'ning bud, and gave ye Names,
Who now shall rear ye to the Sun . . .

. . . .
. . . from thee
How shall I part, and whither wander down
Into a lower World, to this obscure
And wild . . . (XI, 273-84).

Now the light of high noon is a pitiless revelation of man's and Satan's disobedience, so that the Serpent "Back to the Thicket slunk" (784), and Adam newly-terrified, with eyes opened to the light of experience, cries out:

> . . . O might I here
> In solitude live . . .
> Obscur'd, where highest Woods impenetrable
> To starr or Sun-light, spread thir umbrage broad
> And brown as Evening: Cover me ye Pines,
>
> . . . .
>
> Hide me, where I may never see them more (1084-90).

But we know that there is only one scene in all of creation which fits his description: the palpable obscure of hell.

At this point, Adam feels that the second fall, like the first, has been from brightness into the hopeless darkness of hell. He verbally echoes Satan's earlier despair (IV, 76-7) as he cries:

> . . . into what Abyss of fears
> And horrors hast thou driv'n me; out of which
> I find no way, from deep to deeper plung'd!
> Thus *Adam* to himself lamented loud
> Through the still Night . . .
> . . . with black Air
> Accompanied, with damps and dreadful gloom (X, 842-8).

But if so it seems to the father of mankind, the reader understands that the final resurgence into light has already begun. The language of Book Ten is a thicker network of vertical movement than we have met since the books describing hell. As man falls, "Th' Angelic Guards ascended" (X, 18) to report the act with "dim sadness" (23) in heaven. This is the cue for Christ's promised sacrifice, and immediately "Down he descended straight" (90). The sun lowers with him in parallel descent.

> Now was the Sun in Western cadence low
> From Noon, and gentle Airs due at thir hour
> To fan the Earth now wak'd, and usher in
> The Ev'ning cool when he from wrath more cool
> Came the mild Judge and Intercessor both
> To sentence Man . . . (92-7).

Scriptural, the evening hour is not unrelated to the symbolism of high noon. Augustine had continued in his exposition of the *daemonio meridiano*: "Quare autem in meridie? Quia multum fervet persecutio: majores aestus dixit meridiem."[60] But perhaps Milton's comment on how the fall acted by "carnal desire enflaming" is even better glossed by Bishop Babington's explanation of Christ's coming in the evening of the fatal day: "Agayne by *the coole of the day*, we may note if wee will the opportunitie of tyme that God tooke to come to doo good vpon these seduced sinners, to wit, when the heate of the temptation was past . . . that is, when wofull experience hath beate vs, and sinfull heate is abated in vs."[61]

This descent of the Son is projected into the eternal future of which history is the type in the poet's interpolation concerning how Satan falls

> . . . like Lightning down from Heav'n,
> Prince of the Air; then rising from his Grave
> Spoil'd Principalities and Powers, triumpht

---

[60] Augustine *Enarrationes in Psalmos* xc. 8. He goes on to associate the *daemonio meridiano* with the pressures upon pseudo-martyrs who deny their Christianity under torture.

[61] Gervase Babington, *Certaine Plaine, briefe, and comfortable Notes, vpon every Chapter of Genesis* (London, 1596), p. 37.

In open show, and with ascension bright
Captivity led captive through the Air (X, 184-88).

And almost at once Christ in the present leaves man while "with swift ascent he up return'd . . . in glory" (224-6).

Even as he rises into the heavens again, there is an infernal parody, almost the last, as Sin and Death rise along their highway toward the world and meet "*Satan* in likeness of an Angel bright" steering his course while Christ's counterpart "the Sun in *Aries* rose" (327-9). When he "saw descend / The Son of God" he hid, only to return "By Night" to eavesdrop on the consequences of that act which had begun in his earlier midnight enchantments in Eve's dream (337-45). Now "the Prince of Darkness" (383), he urges Sin and Death on to Paradise "while I / Descend through Darkness" to report in hell "this glorious Work" (391-4). Once in hell, the descriptions of inner and outward status seem to involve Satan in a frenzy of revolving, endless movement. If he "Ascended his high Throne," "Down a while / He sat." If he is "fulgent," if once again old Lucifer in "shape Star-bright appear'd," it is with bathetic "permissive glory," all that "since his fall / Was left him, or false glitter" (445-52). Then it is over. Having boasted of his accomplishments, Satan ends his oration with a rhetorical question: "What remains, ye Gods, / But up and enter now into full bliss" (502-3). The answer comes with terrible swiftness as "down he fell / A monstrous Serpent on his Belly prone" (513-4); we have seen how the other demons too crash upon the ground after tumbling down the chain of being into the groveling guise of the serpent. We will see no more of Satan nor of Christ: their antipodal journeys to the high throne and the bottomless pit have climaxed: the one in harmony, the other in discord, reminding us of that great summary line which taught that "rising or falling still advance his praise."

But this *concordia discors* is an eternal triumph; it is not so in nature. Here the fallen parents "hid in gloomiest shade" (716) look out across "the still Night . . . and dreadful gloom" (847-9) to see before them only "a long day's dying" (964). And crazed nature parodies the paradoxical harmony of eternity, for here the planets learn "which of them rising with the Sun, or falling, / Should prove tempestuous" (663-4). The sun is terrible, so for Adam is the cold night (1069-70); rising and falling, sun and star, night and day, God and Satan seem now the environing enemies of man.

But Adam is staring into the nightmare future of a fallen nature. The closing books open, "after sleepless Night" (XI, 173), with the final morning in paradise, replete immediately with promise when "To resalute the World with sacred Light / *Leucóthea* wak'd" (134-5). It is the last temporal shifting of the light and dark setting; this morning persists through the close of the work, properly (and yet not without its complex epicycles) because that close will only be reached after Adam's inner eye has been opened to see through the darkness of fallen creation to the glorious spiritual resurrection which God's paradoxical logic can derive from it.

It is the pattern of vertical movement which continues to dominate both action and language in the last books, to such an extent that the Garden landscape disappears almost entirely in the surging motion.[62] But if we are to realize how closely the vertical pattern is correspondent in its nuances to the curve of the argument, it is necessary to pause for some general distinctions. The vertical pattern in Book Ten has been more than usually unambiguous as physical movement through space, a properly tangible emphasis in that section of the epic which recounts the immediate results of the fall with special reference to man, hell and nature — the levels of creation. In contrast,

[62] J. B. Broadbent, "Milton's Paradise," *MP*, LI (1954), 160-76, observes the disappearance of the Garden from the last books and makes interesting comments upon descriptive techniques and sources.

the vertical imagery of the final books is less physical, more inward, than usual, as the poem turns from history to vision,
and through vision orients itself from time toward eternity.
Further, Book Eleven, reviewing the decline suffered through
the first generations, is honeycombed with a downward movement, while Book Twelve, repository of the exfoliated landscape of the fortunate fall, moves upward until the closing lines
which describe the return to the beginning of the journey upward, the last version of the descent into resurrection.

At the opening of the Eleventh Book, Adam and Eve are
found where:

> . . . they in lowliest plight repentant stood
> Praying, for from the Mercy-seat above
> Prevenient Grace descending had remov'd
> The stony from thir hearts . . . (XI, 1-4).

It is the fortunate fall in little; the grace descending made it
possible that "thir prayers / Flew up," "wing'd for Heav'n with
speedier flight" (5-20). Adam knows that "The good which we
enjoy, from Heav'n descends; / But that from us aught should
ascend to Heav'n" which could concern God he cannot yet
realize (142-6). The remorse and penitence grow stronger as
Adam and Eve watch animate nature, in contrast with its rising
creation in Book Seven, enter upon discord as have the planets,
in a swooping rush which images the fall before their eyes:

> . . . nigh in her sight
> The Bird of *Jove,* stoopt from his aery tow'r,
> Two Birds of gayest plume before him drove:
> Down from a Hill the Beast that reigns in Woods,
> First hunter then, pursu'd a gentle brace (184-8).

At this juncture, Michael comes:

> . . . in the East
> Darkness ere Day's mid-course, and Morning light
> More orient in yon Western Cloud that draws
> O'er the blue Firmament a radiant white,
> And slow descends, with something heav'nly fraught (203-7).

The ambiguous confusion of light and darkness in the coming is analogue to that which shadows the close of the poem in the guardianship of the eastern gate of paradise, image of the inherent ambiguity "Betwixt the world destroy'd and world restor'd," the former already seen, the latter to be promised in the angelic consolation now begun.

Soon Eve laments her destiny by which she must "wander down / Into a lower World, to this obscure" (282-3); Adam laments: "In yonder nether World where shall I seek / . . . bright appearances" (328-9), when Michael affirms that "this pre-eminence thou hast lost, brought down / To dwell on even ground now with thy Sons" (347-8).

Then the crosscurrent sweeps the surface of sorrow as Michael leads Adam toward his vision, commanding "Ascend / This Hill," and Adam gratefully responds "Ascend, I follow thee" (366-71). "So," cries Milton, "both ascend / In the visions of God" (376-7). The vision is, of course, a glimpse into the abyss before the life-giving entrance of Christ into the divine plan. And for one Enoch, "rising, eminent / In wise deport," when "a Cloud descending snatch'd him thence" (665-71), there are thousands of Sethites, who (like their ultimate progenitors) "From the high neighbouring Hills, which was thir Seat, / Down to the Plain descended" (575-6) into sin. Book Eleven closes its vision with Noah, and the account of the Flood is a symphony of rising and falling rhythms, a symphony appropriate to the history of "the only Son of light / In a dark Age" (808-9). It rains "day and night," the "Deep / Broke up," paradise is swept "Down the great River to the op'ning

Gulf," the ark is "Fast on the top of some high mountain fixt," but "The ancient Sire descends" with "uplifted hands," and in answer to his prayers "God voutsafes to raise another World / From him" (825-78).

In dividing the last book of his epic, Milton added three opening lines which echo all the way back to the noon measure of Mulciber's fall, but now with a new vantage-point from which to view the fall — that of God's paradox. Michael pauses in his account,

> As one who in his journey bates at Noon,
> Though bent on speed, so here the Archangel paus'd
> Betwixt the world destroy'd and world restor'd (XII, 1-3).

Adam hears account, then,[63] of how man, in falsely aspiring, parodies hell, even as hell in its aspirations had parodied heaven. Nimrod, like Satan, "shall rise / Of proud ambitious heart" (24-5), and his rebel crew shall build an edifice which, recalling Pandemonium, is constructed of "a black bituminous gurge" that "Boils out from under ground, the mouth of Hell" (41-2). The ambition, of course, is infernal — "to build / A City and Tow'r, whose top may reach to Heav'n" (43-4). The commentary reflects Adam's experience of spatial and spiritual ironies: he now knows that when man would "aspire / Above his Brethren," although he attempts to "Obstruct Heav'n Tow'rs," the result can only be as Michael phrases it: "Nations will decline so low / From virtue" (64-5, 52, 97-8).

When ultimately the narrative leaves the world destroyed for the world restored by Christ's intercession, Adam ecstatically thanks Michael as the "Enlight'ner of my darkness," through

---

[63] Broadbent, *Some Graver Subject,* pp. 276-8, notes that "Michael is in fact preaching a 17th-century sermon of the plain Puritan kind" (p. 276). Broadbent's strictures upon the "moral" ignore the position of the sermon in the context of symbolic epic.

whom "I find / Mine eyes true op'ning, and my heart much eas'd" (271-4); this is a final link in the chain of blindness-and-sight imagery which fits triumphantly into the pattern of noonday light. Earlier, God had declared that he would clear for the willing "thir senses dark," that they might see the "Light after light" of his "day of grace" (III, 188-98). And Adam finally has turned from the terror of the convictive light of nature's noon into God's light. "Now," he affirms, "I see / His day" (276-7). Vision has at last arisen out of darkness. The first paradox has completed its course.

Swiftly follows Michael's account of Christ's ultimate judgment of the world and the pit, of how after death "ere the third dawning light / Return, the Stars of Morn shall see him rise / . . . fresh as the dawning light" (421-3). In ascending "triúmphing through the air," Christ will fix "far deeper" in the head of Satan the sting of death (432, 451-2), then he will forever "enter into glory, and resume / His Seat at God's right hand, exalted high / Above all names in Heav'n" (456-8).

In this history Adam has seen the high noon of eternity when "All in All" rests in climactic brilliance at the peak of eternity. It remains only for Adam to translate the argument of all the epic into the pattern of rising light. "More wonderful" this paradox, exults Adam,

> Than that which by creation first brought forth
> Light out of darkness! full of doubt I stand
> Whether I should repent me now of sin
> By mee done and occasion'd, or rejoice
> Much more, that much more good thereof shall spring (471-6).

The patterns of ascent and luminosity have culminated with the culmination of the argument they have enacted. Adam has been blinded to attain insight; God first created physical light out of "old Night," now he has in a second creation made spiritual light emerge from the darkness of the fallen soul.[64]

And yet, this vision is of a future without time, while the epic lies within a history which must change the poet's "Notes to Tragic." So, at the close, the fall promises felicity, but also that pain and death toward which the language rushes downward. "Let us descend now . . . from this top / Of Speculation" commands Michael in response to Adam's penitent joy. "He ended, and they both descend the Hill; / Descended, *Adam* to the Bow'r where *Eve* / Lay sleeping ran" (588-9, 606-8). "All in bright array / The Cherubim descended," and Michael hurries Adam and Eve "down the Cliff as fast / To the subjected Plain" (627-8, 639-40). Evening closes over a world in which the light becomes a vivid recollection of the hell with which the poem began:

> They looking back, all th' Eastern side beheld
> Of Paradise, so late thir happy seat,
> Wav'd over by that flaming Brand, the Gate
> With dreadful Faces throng'd and fiery Arms (641-4).[65]

And yet, if the gate is shimmering with a terrible light descended as a "Darkness ere Day's mid-course," Adam has learned now that, paradoxically, the real gate is merely the metaphor, that "to the faithful Death [is] the Gate of Life" (571). Man fallen has been caught in the glorious hands of Providence, whence he shall rise again, "Whether in Heav'n or Earth, for then the Earth /

---

[64] Cf. *De doctrina*: ". . . the end which a sinner has in view is generally something evil and unjust, from which God uniformly educes a good and just result, thus as it were creating light out of darkness" (*CE*, XV, 75).

[65] Svendsen, *Milton and Science*, pp. 105-13, has brilliantly analyzed the imagery of mists and exhalations which is used repeatedly in describing Satan, and which reappears at this point (628-32) to enforce the ambiguous Satan-guardian likeness. But cf. also I, 595; V, 185; IX, 74-5; X, 694-5; XI, 740-5.

Shall all be Paradise, far happier place / Than this of *Eden*" (463-5). The journey is long before them, across a darkling plain, but the glory of eternity illumines all within for the author of the epic and the author of us all.

V

THE CREATING
VOICE

I

Muse and Poet in "Paradise Lost"

IN THIS CHAPTER I wish to consider two important sections of *Paradise Lost* which have perennially attracted critical and historical commentary, in the hope that read against the background of the earlier discussion of metaphoric structure in the epic they may yield somewhat richer harmonies than have yet been heard by their commentators.

The problem of identifying the muse in *Paradise Lost* has been attacked with learning and analytical sophistication of a high order in recent years.[1] If the event has not been entirely

[1] It is my impression that the main stream of theological analysis runs from Denis Saurat's English revision (*Milton: Man and Thinker* [New York, 1925]), which presented the Holy Spirit as undogmatic and even superfluous myth, through Harris Fletcher's insistence upon Semitic sources (*Milton's Semitic Studies and Some Manifestations of Them in His Poetry* [Chicago, 1926] and *Milton's Rabbinical Readings* [Urbana, Ill., 1930]) to Maurice Kelley's rebuttal in *This Great Argument*, with important literary tributaries brought to bear in the implications of Lily Bess Campbell's "The Christian

conclusive, still Maurice Kelley apparently sums up orthodoxy for most recent readers when he concludes:

> I am disposed to find no contradiction between the theory of
> the *De doctrina* and the practice of *Paradise Lost,* and to suggest,
> consequently, that when John Milton sought divine guidance
> for his supreme poetical effort, he addressed a muse who is
> separate and apart from the Third Person of the Trinity. In-
> fluenced by his anti-Trinitarian dogma . . . he invoked a per-
> sonification of the various attributes of God the Father, and thus
> turned for inspiration and knowledge not to what he considered
> a subordinate figure but rather to the Father himself — the very
> fountainhead of all wisdom and enlightenment.[2]

Recent studies of the invocation of Book Three, showing good
evidence for the "holy Light" there addressed being Christ,[3]
complicate this summary, but do not contradict it, since the *De
doctrina* associates the Spirit not only with the Father but with
Christ. However, even in accepting the general direction proposed by Kelley's conclusion, one is drawn to admit that the very
multiplicity of definitions which allows the same Spirit-muse to
reconcile aspects of both Father and Son also makes the discussion in *De doctrina* so unsatisfying dogmatically. In his
theological epitome, Milton, as so often, is organizing Scripture

---

Muse," *HLB*, VIII (1935), 29-70, and (less convincingly) Courtland D.
Baker's "Certain Religious Elements in the English Doctrine of the Inspired
Poet During the Renaissance," *ELH*, VI (1939), 300-23. George N. Conklin
has given Kelley general support against both Fletcher and the Lewisite re-
action in a study which, however, eschews analysis of *Paradise Lost* (*Biblical
Criticism and Heresy in Milton* [New York, 1949]).

[2] Kelley, *This Great Argument*, pp. 117-8. Cf. his careful analysis, pp. 106-
18, but also the proviso that perhaps "he never thought of his Muse in
theological terms, that he never consciously connected Urania with any of the
dogma so carefully detailed in the pages of the *De doctrina Christiana*"
(p. 116).

[3] W. B. Hunter, Jr., "Holy Light in 'Paradise Lost,'" and J. H. Adamson,
"Milton's Arianism." See above, p. 106.

toward a negative definition: he presents an attack upon Trinitarianism where one seeks in vain for a clear and positive identification of the Holy Spirit. Not only is the resulting lack of precision foreign to the methods of *Paradise Lost,* but, since the muse is addressed largely in light imagery which becomes necessarily involved with the basic structuring of light symbolism in the body of the epic, clarity may be expected to arise from the pressures of the entire poem. Perhaps it is best, then, to put our questions concerning the muse first to the poet, rather than the theologian.

The initial phase of the initial invocation is unambiguously addressed to the

> . . . Heav'nly Muse, that on the secret top
> Of *Oreb* or of *Sinai,* didst inspire
> That Shepherd, who first taught the chosen Seed,
> In the Beginning how the Heav'ns and Earth
> Rose out of *Chaos* . . . (I, 6-10).

This is thematically appropriate, since the muse is to aid in singing again Moses' myth: the disobedience, the fall into woe and loss of Eden.[4] But this poem embraces the paradox of resurrection, and so it is also appropriate that the invocation immediately begins that vertical movement upward which is so fundamental to the entire argument and edifice: we begin "on the top" a history of how the creation "rose" — as it will be seen rising in Book Seven.

The next phase seems to offer an alternative:

> . . . or if *Sion* Hill
> Delight thee more, and *Siloa's* Brook that flow'd

---

[4] I read "till one greater Man / Restore us, and regain the blissful Seat" as defining the duration of "our woe," not as setting a terminus for the history which the muse is called upon to inspire.

Fast by the Oracle of God; I thence
Invoke thy aid to my advent'rous Song,
That with no middle flight intends to soar
Above th' *Aonian* Mount, while it pursues
Things unattempted yet in Prose or Rhyme (10-6).

It is an alternative chosen to enhance the complexity of suggestion through precise, but suppressed, allusions. Hesiod, Milton's
reader would recollect, studs the opening pages of the *Theogony*
with pictures of the Muses dancing on Helicon "about the deep-
blue spring and altar of the almighty son of Cronos."[5] Milton
emphasizes a parallel physical situation in the world of Jerusalem's sweet singers, where Siloa flows "Fast by" the temple of
Mount Sion, then calls up the recollection by reference to "th'
Aonian Mount."[6] But the parallel is discarded even as it is being
suggested: if Milton's muse may delight in a scene like that
on Helicon, it demands a transcendent discrepancy in the harmony that will emanate from the two worlds — a point made
through the continued vertical movement of the "flight" beyond myth.

This is a cogent and accurate description of one way in which
the passage works, but one which makes fewer demands upon
the lines than they will serve, and which stops short of the
critical allusion. Siloa appears in only four scattered places of
Scripture, yet it emerges in the two central invocations of *Paradise Lost*. Two of the references to Siloa (Σιλωά or Σιλωάμ) are
entirely negligible: Nehemiah 3:15 mentions "the wall of the
pool of Siloah" among the repairs made by the builders of
the wall; Luke 13:4 mentions an unidentified "tower in Siloam"
which fell. Isaiah 8:6 seems to set "the waters of Shiloah that go
softly" against "the waters of the river strong and many, even
the King of Assyria" as a symbolic warning. None of these

[5] *Theogonia*, ed. with an English trans. by Hugh G. Evelyn-White (London, 1914), lines 1-25, 36-9, 50-2, 53-115.
[6] This interpretation, perhaps first adumbrated by Masson, has been most
effectively stated by A. W. Verity, *Paradise Lost* (Cambridge, 1936), II, 369.

passages much distinguishes Siloa among the towers and walls, the rivers and pools, of Jerusalem. The Gospel of John contains the final reference in the ninth chapter. Christ, in healing the man blind from birth, first anointed his eyes, then "said unto him, Go, wash in the pool of Siloam (which is by the interpretation, Sent). He went his way therefore, and washed, and came seeing." The Pharisees, in questioning the restored man, angrily set Christ against Moses. "Then they reviled him, and said, Thou art his disciple; but we are Moses' disciples." And when he later meets his healed beneficiary, Christ himself creates a symbol from the circumstances: "For judgment I am come into this world, that they which see not might see; and that they which see might be made blind."[7]

The incident caught the attention of Thomas Fuller, who concluded in *A Pisgah Sight of Palestine*:

Amongst the waters merely natural, the fountain or pool of Siloah, with the stream flowing thence into the brook of Kedron, justly claimeth the pre-eminence. Fountain, which both in the name and nature thereof was the lively emblem, if not the real type of our Saviour. Name, which is by interpretation, *sent;* and we know "When the fulness of time was come, God *sent* forth His Son." . . . Nature, for the waters thereof, as a prophet observed, ran softly. . . .

Now, as God was eminently in the still voice (I Kings xix. 12), so also was he effectually once in this still water, when our Saviour sent the blind-born man hither to wash, and thereby he recovered his sight.[8]

[7] John 9:39 is used as a text on "the false conceit of wisdom" in the *De doctrina* (CE, XVII, 32), and John 9:41 is crucial when Milton considers God's ways with the reprobate in the treatise: " 'if ye were blind, ye should have no sin; but now ye say, we see, therefore your sin remaineth'; namely, because your sin is the fruit of pride, not of ignorance" (CE, XIV, 148-9). This can profitably be compared with the commentaries on Eve's noonday fall in ch. IV above. It may also be noted that Milton repeatedly speaks of God's "blinding [excaecando] the understanding" of sinners throughout a long passage in the *De doctrina* (CE, XV, 68, 70, 80).

[8] Thomas Fuller, *A Pisgah Sight of Palestine and the Confines Thereof,*

Robert South made Fuller's "effectually" even more positive in his sermon on the incident, saying: "To cure such a blindness as is born with a man, (as one well observes, and as properly expresses it,) *non artis, sed potestatis est;* it is not a work of skill, but an effect of power; not so much the removing of blindness, as the creating of sight."[9] Tradition, then, suggests that Milton's Siloa allusion not only sets the Hebrew prophetic singers above the pagans, but calls up a scriptural context which exalts Christ over Moses, an exaltation which is directed internally by the comparison of Oreb and Sinai to a Sion and Siloa that may "Delight thee more." But the chief issue, of course, lies in the latent figure of the blind man.

With the next movement of the invocation, the light imagery summons him up through a new contrast:

And chiefly Thou O Spirit, that dost prefer
Before all Temples th' upright heart and pure,
Instruct me, for Thou know'st; Thou from the first
Wast present, and with mighty wings outspread
Dove-like satst brooding on the vast Abyss
And mad'st it pregnant: What in me is dark
Illumine, what is low raise and support;
That to the highth of this great Argument
I may assert Eternal Providence (17-25).

---

with the History of the Old and New Testament Acted Thereon (1650; London, 1869), p. 311. I omit Fuller's citations from Scripture.

[9] *Sermons Preached upon Several Occasions by Robert South* (Oxford, 1842), IV, 391. The patristic tradition behind these contemporary statements can be found gathered in the extensive commentaries of Cornelius a Lapide upon the Johannine chapter. See *Commentarivs in Quatvor Evangelia, avctore R. P. Cornelio Cornelii a Lapide* (Antwerp, 1660), II, 389-98. Especially pertinent is the following: "Quaeres, cur Christus caecum illuminaturus miserit eum ad fontem vel piscinam Siloë? *Resp.* Quia Siloë erat typus Christi, Primo, quia Christus a Patre missus erat in mundum, ad eum luce & doctrina diuina illuminandum, cuius virtute caecus hic illuminabatur, non autem aquarum Siloë vi aut efficacitate, ait S. Chrys. & Irenaeus lib. 4. cap 19" (p. 393).

The vertical movement persists in the request to be "rais'd" to the argument's "highth" (recall the poet's emphatically spatial implication of his "fallen" state at the opening of Book Seven.)[10] And I suggest that it is also present in the image of the upright temple, mirrored toward the close of the First Book by the raising of the temple Pandemonium. Further, throughout the epic, "upright" is a recurrent word carrying an ambiguously spatial orientation, from the open pun of Belial's observation respecting the cannonaded angels, that the new weapons "show us when our foes walk not upright" (VI, 627), to the account of Adam's creation, "not prone / And Brute as other Creatures," but as one who with reason,

> . . . might erect
> His Stature, and upright with Front serene
> Govern the rest . . . (VII, 506-9).[11]

This motif is not relaxed in the following lines which preview what the muse must tell, that is, the "*deep* Tract of Hell," the falling "off" of "highly" favored man, the stirring "up" of envy in a Satan "*aspiring* / To set himself in *Glory above* his Peers" until he "rais'd" war in heaven (27-44; italics mine). And then the narrative begins properly with the next line: "Hurl'd headlong flaming . . . down." Our experience with this narrative has taught us that such vertical emphasis in the imagery invokes concomitant light imagery, and once the implications of Siloa are activated, the lines of invocation receive the influence not only of the poet's own illumination in blindness, but that of his scriptural type in the Gospel, and Christ's words as he healed that blind man with Siloa's brook: "I am the light of the world" — capable, as South insists, of "the creating of sight."

---

[10] Cf. ch. IV, pp. 120-1 above.
[11] Cf. Broadbent, "Milton's Hell," p. 163, on the invocation. For other uses of "upright," generally with literal-conceptual ambiguity, see PL I, 221; II, 72; IV, 837; VI, 82, 270; VII, 632.

There is already a triple movement at work in the poem. Milton is drawing into his primary complex of vertical and light symbols the resonant echoes of scriptural tradition which go so far toward validating the symbolic structures themselves. And he is doubly validating his own prophetic role through the warrant of his scriptural prototype as well as by himself enacting the ascent into light which is the symbolic and narrative end of the poem.

Turning to the invocation of light which opens Book Three, we find the same progression repeated; but now the latent scriptural incident has been drawn much closer to the surface by autobiography. Light is invoked, "since God is light," in images which not only implicate Christ, but indicate his traditional relation with the Father, if Professor Hunter's evidence is accepted. Then the poet's own blindness is acknowledged without despair or recrimination:

> . . . Yet not the more
> Cease I to wander where the Muses haunt
> Clear Spring, or shady Grove, or Sunny Hill,
> Smit with the love of sacred song . . . (III, 26-9).

Down into the shades, or up onto the sunlit hill — the pattern of ascent into light is maintained unambiguously, as the narrative pivots from hell toward heaven, through the offices of the holy light which drew up (and will later be seen drawing up) creation from the abyss, which "didst invest / The rising world of waters dark and deep" (10-11). And if the pastoral idyl at first seems to be enacted on the Aonian Mount, the following qualification leads us back to Siloa:

> . . . but chief
> Thee *Sion* and the flow'ry Brooks beneath
> That wash thy hallow'd feet, and warbling flow,
> Nightly I visit . . . (29-32).

However, these visits do not simply call up Christ's curing of the blind man as the earlier reference to "Siloa's Brook" had done. The allusion rather becomes an implicit contrast against which to view the poet's own permanent blindness described in the preceding lines, with "nightly" a grim but typical pun. With the next lines, incipient bitterness turns to incipient triumph, as the poet finds his nocturnal visits recalling a quartet of blind poet-prophets. And these recollections "voluntary move / Harmonious numbers." The mood shift is made quickly again, however, for these are figures of legend; his own blindness is physical and real, a recognition which returns in a climax of pathetic nostalgia for the lost glories of sight: nature, the "human face divine," and the entrance to wisdom which scientist and Christian apologist alike found in "Nature's works."[12] Bitterness seems again transcendent on this whirligig of reaction only to again, this time with finality, be transcended in a paradox of triumph:

> So much the rather thou Celestial light
> Shine inward, and the mind through all her powers
> Irradiate, there plant eyes, all mist from thence
> Purge and disperse, that I may see and tell
> Of things invisible to mortal sight (51-5).

If "*Sion* and the flow'ry Brooks beneath" have called up Siloa with its cure of the blind man, the blind poet-prophet has also remembered that the physical incident was only the emblem, "if not the real type of our Saviour," and that blindness was not a punishment but a providence for Christ's beneficiary. As South analyzed it in his sermon: ". . . By this unusual providence, Christ takes occasion to dart a beam of saving light into his understanding, and so gave him cause of ever blessing God

---

[12] It will be recalled that this is the scale ascended by the poet on his way to prophetic verse in "Il Penseroso."

for that bodily affliction, which was the happy occasion of such a spiritual deliverence."[13] And this paradox flows into the narrative proper, of course, in that series of vision-in-blindness complexes which culminates in Adam's view of the fortunate fall from Michael's mount of vision.

In both invocations, then, we find that Milton moves from the inspiration of poetry to the inspiration of prophecy, each time turning on the hub of Sion and Siloa, the former to suggest the songs of the Old Testament, the latter to suggest Christ, the "Light of the World."

The poet's allusive structure having shown us Christ where before commentators were prone to see only the prophets, let us turn back to the *De doctrina*. We have earlier noticed that in the chapter *De spiritu sancto*, Milton finds the phrases *spiritus Dei* and *spiritus sanctus* have varying applications throughout Scripture. Of this concept, he observes, "Sometimes it means the light of truth, whether ordinary or extraordinary, wherewith God enlightens and leads his people"; "Sometimes it means that impulse or voice of God by which the prophets were inspired"; "More particularly, it implies that light which was shed on Christ himself"; "It is also used to signify the spiritual gifts

---

[13] *Sermons*, IV, 409. Milton had elaborated this providential theory of blindness in his own person in the *Defensio secunda*: "May I be one of the weakest, provided only in my weakness that immortal and better vigor be put forth with greater effect; provided only in my darkness the light of the divine countenance does but the more brightly shine: for then I shall at once be the weakest and the most mighty; shall be at once blind, and of the most piercing sight. Thus, through this infirmity should I be consummated, perfected; thus, through this darkness should I be enrobed in light. And, in truth, we who are blind, are not the last regarded by the providence of God; who, as we are the less able to discern anything but himself, beholds us with the greater clemency and benignity. . . . The divine law . . . [would not] seem to have brought this darkness upon us so much by inducing a dimness of the eyes, as by the overshadowing of heavenly wings; and not unfrequently is wont to illuminate it again, when produced, by an inward and far surpassing light" (*CE*, VIII, 73; cf. 63-77). The last phrase seems to demand a physical interpretation.

[14] *CE*, XIV, 360-3. Sumner's translations interpolate a continuous light imagery: "Nunc lucem veritatis, sive ordinariam sive extraordinariam, qua

conferred by God on individuals."[14] The main course of the argument then becomes a demonstration that the Spirit is not an independent and necessary third personality of the Trinity, but something better described as "a divine impulse, or light, or voice, or word, transmitted from above either through Christ, who is the Word of God, or by some other channel."[15] Thus, when Milton arrives at Matthew's warning against the unpardonable sin, he can deny the independency of the Holy Ghost and explain that "the words must therefore apply to that illumination, which, as it is highest in degree, so it is last in order of time, whereby the Father enlightens us through the Spirit, and which if any one resist, no method of salvation remains open to him."[16]

The invocations are not vague: they call for that illumination with which God inspired the prophets of the Old Testament, a light which is one with that shed on Christ himself and which was "transmitted through Christ" as cure and symbol to the blind man by Siloa. And in each case the climactic step is a step past history to immediate inspiration: "summa et ordine quidem postrema illuminatione qua pater per spiritum nos illuminat."

Have we drawn any closer to understanding Milton's conception of the muse he invoked than Kelley's study of the *De doctrina* had already taken us? I believe that we have, since now we realize that in the invocation of Book One, as well as in that of Book Three, physical blindness has stood in opposition to spiritual illumination. Nor does the pattern fail in the less elaborate invocations of Books Seven and Nine; the former, where Urania must aid Milton's "mortal voice" that sings "in

suos illuminat Deus atque deducit . . ."; "Nunc illam sive vim sive vocem Dei, quae quoquomodo prophetis inspiratur . . ."; "Etiam qua ipsum Christum . . ."; "In alios etiam dona Dei spiritualia."

[15] CE, XIV, 366-7: "Significat . . . spiritus instinctum, et lucem, et vocem, aut verbum divinum, sive per Christum qui Dei sermo est, sive modo quovis alio divinitus missum."

[16] CE, XIV, 394-7.

darkness" the song first inspired "on the secret top / Of *Oreb* or of *Sinai*," the latter, in which the "Celestial Patroness" deigns her "nightly visitation" to the blind poet in sleep. It is this omnipresence of physical blindness which can lead us to the essence of Milton's muse.

The discussion of the Holy Spirit in *De doctrina*, largely an explanation of what the spirit is not, differs only in elaborateness from Peter Sterry's despair of defining the Spirit: "I can no more convey a sense of the difference [between Reason and Spirit] into any soule, that hath not seen these two Lights shining in it self: than I can convey the difference between Salt and Sugar; to him, who hath never tasted sweet or sharp. These things are discerned only by exercise of senses."

We know that for the Puritan, and more insistently as one moves toward the radical center of Puritanism which Milton inhabits, the Holy Spirit was frequently thought of as a "spiritual perception analogous to the physical perception of the senses and given in 'experience' as a whole."[17] It has been the burden of another chapter to demonstrate that metaphoric tradition made it inevitable that most spiritual discussion should be carried on in visual analogy, and Puritanism was no exception. Thomas Goodwin, for example, elaborately developed the perceptual analogy through the vehicle of a man born in darkness emerging by degrees into the brightest glory of the sun:

> Suppose any one of the sons of men brought up in those *merae tenebrae*, mere darkness which were only nature's legacy, and on the sudden God should set up in the lantern of his brains the light of the greatest magnitude that Plato or Socrates ever had, how would this man bless himself . . . then let this man be carried forth into the open sky, and let anyone shew him a full moon, walking in her greatest brightness, as Job speaks, Oh, how would he kiss his hand to it, and passionately cry out, Oh,

[17] Geoffrey Nuttall, *The Holy Spirit in Puritan Thought and Experience* (Oxford, 1946), p. 38. The previous quotation from Sterry appears on p. 39.

this is light, this is day indeed. . . . anon when the day is approaching let him discover the twinkling stars to close up their
lights and vanish, and the brightness to wash off by degrees from
his so adored moon, which he verily took for the sun, and her
face to grow pale and wan, and a far differing, stronger light to
steal in by degrees . . . till at last casting his eye to that quarter
of heaven which is brightest, he discerns the body of the sun
beginning to peep up above the horizon — do but think with your-
selves, upon the sight hereof, what this man would say.[18]

We have earlier discussed at some length how such ideas,
theological conceptions though they are, are so refractory in
an abstract context that Milton's insistence in *De doctrina*
upon the Holy Spirit as "a divine impulse, or light, or voice,
or word" joins the Quaker incantations or the Platonists' "Candle
of the Lord" in frustrating the dogmatic theologian who tries
to grasp their protean elusiveness for either argument or analysis.
So long as we insist upon making poetry into theology, insist
upon turning to the *De doctrina* to define symbols which are
gradual developments within the poem's metaphoric structure,
so long will we be frustrated in hearing Milton's harmonies.

The blind man of Jerusalem was given a physical affliction
which led to a spiritual awakening. But his physical vision was
also created anew in the miracle, and it is this "felt" sight which
Milton recalls in order to define as well as to symbolize his own
"spiritual perception analogous to the physical perception of the
senses."

Let us approach the problem with another touchstone so that
it can reveal to us one final and further realization about the
pattern of Milton's epic. Torquato Tasso's *Le Sette Giornate del
Mondo Creato* was published posthumously in 1607. There has
been some debate concerning its influence upon Milton, and I

[18] Ibid., pp. 40-1. Nuttall examines the tradition of light imagery for the
Spirit in pp. 39-47.

am inclined to believe that it had little, if any.[19] But a brief stylistic comparison appears no less valuable in either case.

Il Mondo Creato, inspired by Tasso's urge to identify himself with the wave of authoritarian devotionalism which swept Italy at the peak of the Counter-Reformation, reveals a nontheological mind attempting to center an hexameral poem theologically by arguing the usual questions on the source of matter, or the plurality of worlds, by reference to the schoolmen and the most orthodox patristic commentators. It is a dogmatic poem, and its dogmatism is peculiarly reflected in the opening invocation:

> Padre del Cielo, e tu del Padre eterno
> Eterno Figlio, e non creata prole,
> De l'immutabil mente unico parto:
> Divina imago, al tuo divino essempio
> Eguale; e lume pur di lume ardente;
> E tu, che d'ambo spiri, e d'ambo splendi,
> O di gemina luce acceso Spirto,
> Che sei pur sacro lume, a sacra fiamma,
> Quasi lucido rivo in chiaro fonte,
> E vera imago ancor di vera imago,
> In cui se stessa il primo essempio agguaglia,
> (Se dir conviensi) e triplicato Sole,
> Che l'alme accendi, e i puri ingegni illustri;
> Santo don, santo messo, e santo nodo,
> Che tre Sante Persone in un congiungi,
> Dio non solingo, in cui s'aduna il tutto,
> Che 'n varie parti poi si scema, e sparge:
> Termine d'infinito alto consiglio,
> E de l'ordine suo Divino Amore;

[19] F. T. Prince, *The Italian Element in Milton's Verse* (Oxford, 1954), pp. 34-57, finds *Il Mondo Creato* to be an exemplar of Tasso's ideal style for heroic verse, the first ambitious nondramatic venture in *versi sciolti*, and, therefore, an important model for Milton, whose interest in Tasso's theory of epic styles is indubitable. But Mario Praz, *The Flaming Heart* (Garden City, 1958), pp. 320-31 debilitates Prince's large claims. Broadbent, *Some Graver Subject*, pp. 140-1, is cursory.

Tu dal Padre, e dal Figlio in me discendi,
E nel mio core alberga, e quinci e quindi
Porta le grazie, e inspira i sensi e i carmi,
Perch'io canti quel primo alto lavoro,
Ch'è da voi fatto, e fuor di voi risplende
Maraviglioso, e 'l magistero adorno
Di questo allor da voi creato mondo,
In sei giorni distinto. . . .[20]

The numerous parallels between this invocation and those at
the opening of the First and the Third Books of *Paradise Lost*
serve only to emphasize a fundamental difference which "places"
the narrator in the economy of the later epic. In "l'alme accendi,
e i puri ingegni illustri" Tasso's plurals immediately abolish the
poet's uniqueness, qualify, by dividing, his prophetic status. More
important is the structuring of the catalogue of images for the
Spirit itself. There is an immediate drive toward intensification
of the brilliance in the opening lines from "lume pur di lume
ardente" through the superimposition of "vera imago ancor di
vera imago." The intensity, however, is handled astructurally
if this is to be read literally as an invoking of the Spirit for the
singing of the "primo alto lavoro," because the light paradoxes
fall off following these lines into discursive theological description of the Spirit's duties rather than its essence, so that when
one arrives at the poet's personal nexus with the inspiring light,
all power is spent. The point could scarcely be emphasized more
clearly than by the poet's logic that he needs illumination because he wishes to sing.

Milton is both more demanding and assertive: he sings because
he is inspired. In his first invocation he achieves climactic intensity when he initially unites the light and vertical patterns
which will govern his poem precisely at that point in which the

---

[20] Torquato Tasso, *Il Mondo Creato*, edizione critica con introduzione e
note di Giorgio Petrocchi (Florence, 1951), *Primo Giorno*, 1-27.

Spirit and the prophetic soul of the poet meet: "What in me is dark / Illumine, what is low raise and support" (22-3). If he requests clarity of inner vision, he has already commanded the heavenly muse to sing, already epitomized his "advent'rous Song." The confidence is validated by the transformation of autobiography into symbol. In his own person Milton finds summarized the great argument of light coming out of darkness through the rise of fallen man, "on evil days though fall'n, and evil tongues," because he is blind. It is this blindness which makes him the proper vehicle for the muse; and as he summons up "Blind *Thamyris* and blind *Maeonides*, / And *Tiresias* and *Phineus* Prophets old" (III, 34-5), as he summons up the symbolic blind man at Siloa, he himself joins them as a mythic type both embracing and giving verisimilitude to his narrative. It is in the light of this status that we can discover the profoundest significance of the vision-in-blindness scenes throughout the epic. For in the chronology of the symbolic structure, it is Milton the inspired narrator who is authenticated by his blindness as primal prophet: the breathing type and tangible continuity of Michael who prophesied the future for a miraculously blinded Adam; of God who, dark with his own brightness, prophesies the mythic circle of the fortunate fall which will bring to all men of good will, as it has already brought to the illuminated poet, light out of darkness.

II

Milton's Rhetoric of Paradox:

The Dialogue in Heaven

IF WE TURN now to the prophet-God of *Paradise Lost*, it will perhaps seem appropriate to do so through the prophet-poet's invocation to light in Book Three. We have examined this invocation from one point of vantage; from another we may say that it is a "dialogue" of metaphoric definition, introductory to the dialogue in heaven which immediately follows.

But it is a dialogue without a respondent, the auditor's presence being implied as the speaker defines him interrogatively ("May I express thee unblam'd," "Or hear'st thou rather"), until ultimately he admits, "Thee I revisit safe with bolder wing" (3-13). Such univocal dialogue resulted not uncommonly from Ramism: "in the characteristic outlook fostered by the Ramist rhetoric, the speaking is directed to a world where even persons respond only as objects — that is, say nothing back."[21] But the speaker's definition of the auditor is clear in spite of his alternative attempts to express it: the implied respondent is *visibility, light*. And this respondent of the invocative dialogue becomes the directing speaker of the major dialogue, "since God is light." The definition is visual, and yet there is an extraordinary synesthesic effect here: it was "the *voice* of God" which called up into light and being "The rising world of waters dark and deep." And the poet's creation is imitative of the deity's as he rises "with bolder wing" into "flight / Through utter and through middle darkness," up into the light of "thy sovran . . . Lamp," but he rises through *voice* ("I sung of *Chaos*") to *vision*, "that I may see and tell" (11-22, 54).[22]

In this invocation we also may notice a somewhat heightened style: insistent and pressing rhetorical schemes emerge immediately in those descriptive revisions of identification which the poet applies to the Spirit. "Correction," says Thomas Wilson in *The Arte of Rhetorique*, "is when we alter a word or sentence, otherwise than we haue spoken before, purposing thereby to aug-

---

[21] Ong, *Ramus*, p. 287.
[22] Instructive at this point is Arnold Stein's brief but incisive discussion of the historical relationship between sight and sound values, between theories of light and of harmony, in the Renaissance background: *Answerable Style*, pp. 151-4.

ment the matter, and to make it appeare more vehement." Milton's "correction" is crossed with that allied scheme of which Wilson says: "Doubtfulnesse is then vsed, when we make the hearers beleeue that the weight of our matter causeth vs to doubt what were best to speake."[23]

The major rhetorical technique, however, is repetition, first in the several synecdochic reapplications of the metaphor "light," but most noticeably in the smaller sound play of "I revisit now," "I revisit safe," "Revisit'st not these eyes," to "Nightly I visit." And this repetition draws attention to itself more readily by being caught up in an epanalepsis, "when ye make one worde both beginne and end your verse, which therefore I call the slow retourne," explains Puttenham:[24]

> . . . thee I revisit safe,
> And feel thy sovran vital Lamp; but thou
> Revisit'st not these eyes . . . (21-3).

And the schematic structure of this *serpentina carmina* is repeated a few lines later:

> Those other two equall'd with me in Fate,
> So were I equall'd with them in renown (33-4).

---

[23] Thomas Wilson, *The Arte of Rhetorique* (1560), ed. G. H. Mair (Oxford, 1909), pp. 185-6.

[24] George Puttenham, *The Arte of English Poesie* (1589), ed. Gladys D. Willcock and Alice Walker (Cambridge, 1936), p. 200. It may be objected that the passage does not precisely conform to Puttenham's definition or examples, but Abraham Fraunce (*The Arcadian Rhetoricke* [1588], ed. Ethel Seaton [Oxford, 1950], p. 60) used the term for an exactly similar construction: "There be some called *Serpentina carmina*, because they turne and winde themselues *in orbem* like a snake, and their only grace proceedeth from a Rhetoricall *Epanalepsis*: as those in Ouid,

> *Vna dies Fabios ad bellum miserat omnes,*
> *Ad bellum missos perdidit una dies.*"

Lines fifty-six through seventy-nine constitute a transition between dialogues in which the poet describes God, his setting and his actions. And God is visile again here; in keeping with the light and blindness motifs of the invocation, he is an "eye." Yet he is being prepared as a voice, and if the eye is a visual symbol, it is the only visible characteristic, and it transforms pseudo-synesthetically into an echo of the poet's desire to "see and tell" when the transition passage closes on the statement that God "foreseeing spake."

The dialogue in heaven has never been a popular section of *Paradise Lost,* and Arnold Stein's comment that "Language and cadence are as unsensuous as if Milton were writing a model for the Royal Society and attempting to speak purely to the understanding" is characteristic.[25] Recently an attempt was made to salvage the heavenly dialogue by arguing that it is a dramatic encounter universalizing the freedom of will through the act of a Son ignorant of the ultimate structure of the eternal myth.[26] This defender has attempted to defeat Stein's sort of objection through a strategy of encirclement, admitting the fact but providing a new rationale:

The near tonelessness of his [God's] first speech at once proves itself the right tone. . . . For the omniscient voice of the omnipotent moral law speaks simply what is. Here is no orator using rhetoric to persuade, but the nature of things expounding itself in order to present fact and principle unadorned.[27]

---

[25] *Answerable Style,* p. 128; for a similiar comment one can turn to Rajan's recent compendium of rather standard reactions, *Paradise Lost and the Seventeenth Century Reader,* pp. 128-30. Coleridge in speaking for the defense could only say that Milton "slips in, as it were by stealth, language of affection, or thought, or sentiment" (*Coleridge on the Seventeenth Century* ed. Roberta Florence Brinkley [Durham, 1955], p. 590).

[26] Irene Samuel, "The Dialogue in Heaven: A Reconsideration of *Paradise Lost,* III, 1-417," *PMLA,* LXXI (1957), 601-11.

[27] Ibid., p. 603.

This is an impressive defense, but one which blinks the problems of poetry. If God does not use metaphors, yet the poet must use metaphor for God's mode-of-being as for that of the angels; hence it is that God becomes an "eye" by a decorous synecdoche directed by the context of light imagery. This eye of God does not see things metaphorically, but in their essential natures, as Adam saw the natures of the animals when he named them; it is in this perspective that we can best understand what I have elaborated elsewhere — God's vision of history as space and matter. The poet's vision of God's vision can neither deny nor express this quintessential mode of realization. Milton makes his dissolution of the dilemma explicit at the very beginning of the transition from invocation to narrative, revealing that God sees his own creation in the way we have shown that Milton saw the epic. That is, God sees what he has made as simultaneously metaphoric and literal in its reality: the angels, having received beatific glory from "his sight" are "thick as Stars," or Adam and Eve pruning in the garden are "Reaping immortal fruits of joy and love" (III, 60-2, 67). In brief, God sees things as metaphors of their own essence. But he can do so only when he himself becomes a metaphoric "eye," indeed, it is only through this metaphor that one can express God's "vision" at all. But we are nonetheless aware that it is both a decorous and a partial projection to designate as an eye (even as an eye which not only perceives but bathes others creatively in its beams) that being whose essence we know is light.

It can still be insisted, however, that even if the poet can describe God as a synecdochic metaphor viewing synecdochic expressions of that reality he made, God in his own voice can never speak metaphorically. A pair of small points can be observed which make this logical inference into clear poetic implication.

The first is that Sin and Death are not only personified in hell, but in heaven by the Son who, being man, can view and express

them anthropomorphically (III, 241-59). At the same point in
the epic, however, the Father speaks of sin and death conceptually, reducing them from their substantive status to predicates
for man's state of being (203-12). Second, one does find five
"metaphors" in the course of God's speaking. They are all, however, light and dark images, three being patterned into the
promise to clear men's "senses dark," to offer them "Light after
light," but with the effect that the "blind be blinded more" (188-
200). Later he speaks of "golden days, fruitful of golden deeds"
(337), closely reminiscent of the "immortal fruits of joy and
love." But the other instance is the most revealing, constituting
the last (and only apparently metaphorical) word in God's first
speech: "Mercy first and last shall brightest shine" (134). This
line reminds us of the basic premise of the poem's symbolic
structure once again. God *is* the generative "eye" from which
emanates the totality of being, and therefore "shine" is no
metaphor but the essence of mercy, as of all good qualities flowing out from their creative source, for "God is light."

Concerning ourselves with imagery, then, we may find Professor Samuel essentially correct, if we must admit that her
formulation is in danger of cutting some knots with which the
poet-creator is bound to the creator God whom he must express.

But the restriction of metaphor is not the restriction of
rhetoric, and the "unadorned" dialogue in heaven would have
been immediately recognized by any contemporary as one of the
most unflagging and closely-wrought "rhetorical" sections of the
poem.[28] Our contemporary imagistic orientation has blinded us

---

[28] Cf. J. B. Broadbent, "Milton's Rhetoric," *MP*, LVI (1959), 224-42, and
Some Graver Subject, pp. 123, 144-57, for analyses of schematic patterns
with special attention to *Paradise Lost*. Broadbent cites some of the heavenly
dialogue but, since my own readings were made independently, we differ in
particulars. More significantly, my inferences are antithetical to his conclusion
that God's rhetoric cannot support his thematic stature (*Some Graver Subject*, p. 151). However, extremely interesting in the present context is his
comment concerning "iterative schemes": "even after adjusting for different
lengths, Books III and IX stand as the most heavily endowed with this

to this, because the rhetoric here is based in *schemes* rather than *tropes,* figures patterning sounds rather than images; and yet it will be my argument that its ultimate groundwork and justification is tropical. Let us turn now to the details of the dialogue.

When Christ is first viewed (and it is a fact which first renders suspect Professor Samuel's apology for the dialogue as a *drama* of free will in which Christ is not omniscient), his visile presence is also a symbolic presence, presenting a forecast of the aural "argument" he will unfold. Anticipating his role as man, he is not synecdochically presented, in the manner of the Father-eye; but he appears as a "face" just after the Father's utterance of the literal metaphor for mercy: "Mercy first and last shall brightest shine." Now, narrates Milton, "Beyond compare the Son of God was seen / Most glorious, in him all his Father shone," a description which is particularized a moment later when the poet explains that "in his face / Divine compassion visibly appear'd" (138-41). The visile description has already answered the Father's question upon which the whole structure of the fortunate fall must turn: "where shall we find such love / . . . Dwells in all Heaven charity so dear?" (213-6).

Having seen the evidence of the Son's bright countenance, it is clear that this is not the dramatic question which Professor Samuel hears, but a rhetorical question within a ritual of enacted certainty foreshadowing the treatment of temptations in *Paradise Regained.* Further, the language is ritualistic. For Christ not only repeats what the Father has said, but he describes the ritual of repeated worship, that very act which Satan later describes as "The debt immense of endless gratitude, . . . still paying, still to owe" (IV, 52-3):

peculiarly prosodic and verbal kind of rhetoric" ("Milton's Rhetoric," p. 230). This might stand as the logical antipodes to Stein's opinion, cited above, and it is clear that we are in need of a searching and careful analysis. Edward S. LeComte, *Yet Once More: Verbal and Psychological Patterns in Milton* (New York, 1953), pp. 19-47, cites many scattered passages with occasional rhetorical comment.

. . . Man should find grace;
For which both Heav'n and Earth shall high extol
Thy praises, with th' innumerable sound
Of Hymns and sacred Songs, wherewith thy Throne
Encompass'd shall resound thee ever blest (145-9).

And he structures his speech in a variety of reiterative schemes
of alliteration, anaphora ("Should man . . . should man"),
antimetabole ("be from thee far, / That far be from thee") and
epanalepsis ("unmake, / For him, what for thy glory thou hast
made").[29] This seems to me a critical point if we are to understand the impact of this dialogue upon a rhetorically-trained
audience, for Abraham Fraunce no less than Puttenham makes
repetition the basic category for schemes of sound, and Puttenham is quite explicit on the primacy of repetitive schemes:

> And first of all others your figure that worketh by iteration
> or repetition of one word or clause doth much alter and affect
> the eare and also the mynde of the hearer, and therefore is
> counted a very braue figure both with the Poets and rhetori-
> ciens . . .[30]

---

[29] Rhetorical terminology varied, of course. My description of schemes is
drawn primarily from three sources: Puttenham's *Arte of English Poesie*,
John Hoskins' *Directions for Speech and Style* and Abraham Fraunce's
Arcadian Rhetoricke. These offer a cross section, from the conservative Put-
tenham to the Ramistic Fraunce. Where I have found disagreement, I have
consulted Peacham's *Garden of Eloquence;* Wilson's *Arte of Rhetorique;*
Ramus' collaborator's own handbook (*Audomari Talaei rhetorica, e P. Rami
Regii Professoris praelectionibus observata* [Paris, 1572]); and the very useful organization provided in Sister Miriam Joseph's *Shakespeare's Use of the
Arts of Language* (New York, 1947).
  That Milton sometimes complicates the schemes beyond the handbook
descriptions accounts for the fact that there might be alternative labels applied
to some passages; for instance, what I have cited above as antimetabole on
the authority of Hoskins is Puttenham's anadiplosis. It would not aid the
argument to cite particular authorities or terminological disagreements throughout; the point I wish to establish is simply the ubiquitous attention to
schematic forms.
[30] Puttenham, *Arte of English Poesie*, p. 198.

In the Father's response to the Son, he assimilates the latter's rhetoric of repetition. He opens with ploce, or "the doubler," as he plays into a focal position the word "Son" ("O Son, in whom my Soul hath chief delight, / Son of my bosom, Son who art alone / My word" [168-70]), and follows this up with a line featuring "all" in an open epanalepsis: "All hast thou spok'n as my thoughts are, all." Then the typical ambiguity of Milton's language is formed into a triple play upon "will" in the succeeding lines, a paronomasia, which Hoskins explains "is a pleasant touch of the same letter, Sillable, or words, wyth a different meaning."[31] In another moment God imitates his Son in adapting antimetabole ("Upheld by me . . . by me upheld" [178-80]). As he proceeds he turns the ploce, originally applied to the Son, back upon himself, with the patterned repetition of "me," closing the promise of sufficient grace with an anaphora complicated by incorporating what Fraunce called "polyptoton," but which bore the more picturesque designation of "traductio, or the tranlacer" in Puttenham, who explains the structure of such a passage as

To pray, repent, and bring obedience due.
To Prayer, repentance, and obedience due (190-1)

by a simile: "when ye turne and tranlace a word into many sundry shapes as the Tailor doth his garment."[32] Milton would seem to be somewhat abusing epizeuxis with "light after light," "hard be hardn'd," and "blind be blinded" within five lines (196-200), but this is owing to the fact that the speech is approaching its emphatic climax just before the close, and Hoskins explains that epizeuxis "is not to be vsed but in passion."[33] If we view

---

[31] "Directions," in Louise Brown Osborn, *The Life, Letters, and Writings of John Hoskyns* (New Haven, 1937), p. 129.

[32] *Arte*, pp. 203-4.

[33] Osborn, *John Hoskyns*, p. 126.

the "plain style" of God from such a rhetorical standpoint, if we hear these figures as well as the warning anadiplosis of the close when he asserts that "his whole posterity must die, / Die hee or Justice must" (209-10), we are surely prepared to see that Father and Son are acting out, as clearly as Satan and Beelzebub have done in the infernal debates, a rhetorical and nondramatic ritual. From another chain of evidence, then, we are again justified in affirming what the light imagery made clear, that the Father's question, "Dwells in all Heaven charity so dear," is a purely rhetorical question.

Especially does this become clear when the Son responds by applying to himself the Father's own ploce in reiteration of "me";[34] when he opens his response with that particular anadiplosis which Hoskins terms "climax" ("man shall find grace; / And shall grace not find means, that finds her way" [227-8]); when he threads the entire speech with a dominant traduction as he plays all the variant transformations upon the substantive and predicative forms of "death." But the question's suspensive dimension disappears explicitly into the grammatical affirmations of certainty within this response of the Redeemer. "I . . . will," "I shall," he cries, and the Father's acceptance of the offer affirms repeatedly, "thou shalt."

God's reply, in structure, is largely a detailed reiteration of Christ's assertions concerning the results of his own sacrifice — the return of love into eternal joy. This speech by the Father also utilizes schematic figures of repetition, but this time the schemes are not scattered so widely, being drawn together into an incredibly complex rhetorical knot which interweaves within a few lines anaphora, traduction, antistrophe (finishing with like words: "Hellish hate . . . Hellish hate"), and elaborate paronomasia:

[34] Joseph Summers, "The Voice of the Redeemer in *Paradise Lost*," *PMLA*, LXX (1955), 1082-9, demonstrates a complex series of sound-sense echoes of the "me" pattern throughout the epic, revealing a larger repetition of the local schematic figure within the dialogue.

So Heav'nly love shall outdo Hellish hate,
Giving to death, and dying to redeem,
So dearly to redeem what Hellish hate
So easily destroy'd, and still destroys
In those who, when they may, accept not grace (298-302).

It is no fortuitous coincidence that these lines constitute the most explicit statement either speaker has given, in the course of their ritualistic dialogue, to the paradox of the *felix culpa*. For if the rhetorical structure of the Father-Son dialogue is schematic repetition, God and the discourses in heaven employ one great trope. This is schematically emphasized at the very beginning of the dialogue, in God's first speech, when he plays through so elaborate a "tranlacer" upon fall, fell, fallen: the trope is the *paradoxon* of the fortunate fall. Part of the playfulness reflected throughout the poem in the laughter of God, which has given so many readers a shock of sensibility in the context of such high matter, must be accounted for by the fact that all he says is rooted in this grand trope. This inevitably involves that other figure called *ironia*, "The speciall grace whereof," Abraham Fraunce observes, "is in iesting and merie conceipted speaches."[35] This ironic element reminds us that from its formal beginnings in Cicero's *Paradoxa Stoicorum* the genre of paradox involved an element of play. "Ego tibi illa ipsa quae vix in gymnasiis et in otio Stoici probant ludens conieci in communes loci,"[36] explained Cicero in addressing his paradoxes to Brutus, and the persistence of this attitude characterizes the Renaissance paradoxes of Ortensio Lando, Cornwallis or Donne. Quite apart from the inherent influence of irony upon the paradox, the play-

---

[35] *Arcadian Rhetoricke*, p. 10; Henry Peacham, *The Garden of Eloqvence* (London, 1593), pp. 35-6, illustrated *ironia* with God's words: "Behold, the man is become as one of us to know good and euill: by this derision the Lord God reprocheth Adams miserie."

[36] *Paradoxa Stoicorum,* ed. and trans. H. Rackham (London and Cambridge, 1942), p. 256.

ful element within the formal genre could scarcely fail to influence the tropical paradox. But Cicero was also in the tradition of Zeno, of course, and remembered that tripping irony was only a single function of the form, that it was primarily an instrument for revealing truths recalcitrant to syntactical linearity.[37] The writers of formal paradoxes (see, for instance, those issued by John Hall in 1650, or Donne's "That virginity is a vertue" — significantly omitted from the 1633 collection) and the rhetoricians did not always forget this profound epistemological vitality of the trope, as witness Puttenham's description of "paradoxon: or the Wondrer": "Many times our Poet is caried by some occasion to report of a thing that is marvelous, and then he will seeme not to speake it simply but with some signe of admiration."[38]

As the dialogue in heaven unfolds, as God develops the paradox of the fall in his divided persons as Father and Son, Judge and Redeemer, the signs that the audience has reacted in precise accord with Puttenham's expectations are explicitly present: the listening angels are by "Admiration seiz'd" as they stand "Wond'ring" (271, 273).

Both Tuve and Ong have taught us that "ornament" was a means to "illumination" of theme and structure in Renaissance rhetoric and poetic. For the highest speaker of his poem, Milton accordingly employs in the midst of schematic wealth that one trope which is the miniature mimesis of both structure and theme in *Paradise Lost*: paradox. It is appropriate to theme and moment, as well as to speaker, because at this point we are learning the highest paradox, the *felix culpa* which brings "life out of death." And the figure is generically appropriate, too, because

[37] At this point I should like to recall the discussion of the relations between paradox and metaphor, p. 124.

[38] *Arte*, pp. 225-6. Cf. Hoskins (who incorporates *paradoxon* into synoeceosis or "a composition of contraries"): "This is a fine course to stirr admiracon in the hearer & make them thinke it a strange harmonie w[hi]ch must bee exprest in such discords, ... This is an easie figure nowe in fashion not like euer to be soe vsvall" (Osborn, *John Hoskins*, p. 150).

it is a trope which best expresses "wonder," "la meraviglia," that quality which every Renaissance critic advocates as the highest aim of the epic poet.

When the great dialogue is rounded to a close, the poem returns to the voice of the narrating poet, and yet we hear through his voice the angelic choirs: as in the opening invocation which preceded the dialogue, *voice* is leading us once again to the *vision* of God. And with the expression of this vision itself we return in another way to the beginning invocation in which God is light. As the indirectly narrated angelic hymns recapitulate the events just passed, they also catch up the rhetorical modes of the Father and Son, the anadiplosis ("Harps they took, / Harps ever tun'd" [365-66]), the phrase-long ploce ("So strictly, but much more to pity incline" [402, 405]), the climactic anadiplosis on "Love" (410-11). But this is with a fading emphasis, dying echoes from the high moment of *sound* which is now past. The harmony of the dialogue is passing into concord: we see more than we hear. So it is fitting, even structurally inevitable, that the choir should pick up God's great trope, the *paradoxon,* and, in echoing it, should make the culminating vision of God into the great visual paradox from which the metaphoric structure of the epic emanates:

> . . . thee Author of all being,
> Fountain of Light, thyself invisible
> Amidst the glorious brightness where thou sit'st (374-6).

Nowhere else will the blind poet bring forth from the illumination of prophecy a clearer vision of light arising out of darkness.

EPILOGUE

NO COMMENTARY exhausts the values in even a small successful poem; the shelf of commentators will never grow long enough to complete the reading of *Paradise Lost*. If in the course of this book I have often seemed to deny the discoveries of other readers of the poem, it has not been without awareness that my partial truths have been the children of their own. One perceptive reader of an earlier version of this study commented with characteristic good-humored skepticism: "I fail to see in this new Milton, visual master of space, what has finally become of the old poet who used to be master of sound and sensation." I am confident that, if my argument has been worth while, these twin Miltons, separated by the necessary partialness of the critical process when it engages a great poem, will be joined to show us a larger Janus, neither of whose faces will be quite that of the poet we are now prepared to recognize as the author of *Paradise Lost*.

If my reading is but a waypost on the infinite journey man makes in search of the significance of his own words, however, I have tried to argue that it points down the main road of Western thought. Following that road, we have allowed quantification, objectification, the projection of inner states and processes

into a man-constructed world of statistics, charts, machines —
things — , to lead us to the edge of the technological abyss. It has
been known for a long time that the technologists' substitution
of things for men, quantities for irrational values, is rooted in
the history of the seventeenth century. I believe this commonplace is accurate: Ramism, terrifying in its militant campaign to
objectify and to "place" inner experience, history, biography,
man's very temporal being, outside the mind in a cosmos of
bodies and spaces, was a first massive foreshadowing of Ein-
stein's and Minkowski's effective destruction of the barrier which
maintained a dualism between space and time. When that barrier
was finally broken, man had become minion rather than master
of the physical world. It is fitting that the symbol of this changed
relationship should be our own confrontation by the terrible
autonomy of the creatures of our own wills, the strangulation of
the city by the automobile, the mortgaging of the future for the
interplanetary rocket and the intercontinental missile.

But no revolution is without its achievement and its ironies.
My larger historical point has been that this wanton objectifying
movement in European thought — so conveniently focused
around the flourishing of Ramism and its aftermath — produced
an unexpected result when it moved men to objectify words.
For with that attempt the most antipoetical, from one point of
view, of pedagogical systems, became from another, the impetus
for renewed attempts to liberate language in the way poets liberate it. That is, Ramism and the forces which fed into it in the
seventeenth century induced men to leap the aural structures of
syntactical discursion in search of an objective, "corporeal" status
for the word itself, a status in which it would not be a dependent
sign but an immediate creative entity.

If we have seen that this effort cost an unholy price in the
religious struggles of seventeenth-century England, we have also
acknowledged its echoes in the rich critical consciousness of our
own time, and in the great literature which that consciousness

has produced as the aesthetic milieu of the twentieth century, a literature in which time and space coalesce creatively in metaphor and in that extension of metaphor, myth.

But for all of our contemporary wealth, we must still return to the fount. *Paradise Lost,* born in the historical cradle of contemporary sensibilities, remains our richest expression of this metaphoric vision through which man creates his image, daring the spaces and cold infernal dregs of the vast profundity obscure.

Index of Authors